work: 752-6297

Working & Winning With Kids

A Family Affair

Working & Winning With Kids

Suzanne Lindman Hansen

Randall Book
P.O. Box 780
Orem, Utah 84057

©Copyright 1983 by Su-Z Enterprises, Inc.
All rights reserved.
ISBN: 0-934126-31-3
First Printing, March 1983
Randall Book
Orem, Utah
Printed in the United States of America

Acknowledgements

I am truly grateful to my wonderful husband, Michael, for his enthusiastic support of this project; for his countless hours of work, encouragement, and patience in being a daddy, husband, and editor.

I am also grateful to our dear neighbors and friends whose encouragement helped greatly.

Thanks and appreciation for the professional advice and efforts of Susan Southworth, Jay A. Perry, JoAnne Jolley, and Kathy Pitt.

Dedication

To my parents, Wilford and Mary Louise Lindman, whose love and support and encouragement have made all the difference in my life.

And to my enthusiastic children—Jenny, Johnny, Julie—who make motherhood so meaningful and rewarding and down right "FUN."

Contents

	Preface	ix
1.	Making Home Life Better—An Introduction	1
	Section One—Keeping Yourself Motivated	5
2.	It All Starts With You	7
3.	Action Follows Belief	15
4.	Getting the Happiness Habit	21
5.	The Attitude of Gratitude	29
	Section Two—Building Relationships With Your Children, First	37
6.	Getting "Inside" Your Kids	39
7.	Dads Do Make A Difference	47
8.	Raising "I Can" Kids	57
	Section Three—How To Motivate Children To Help in the Home, Happily	67
9.	Incentives Make Things Happen	69
10.	Games That Make Housework Fun	77
11.	More Fun Games	87
12.	Allowance Verses Payday—And Special Awards, Too	97
13.	Easy-to-Make Motivational Charts	111

Preface

I'm probably the most likely individual to write a preface because I've seen the beginning of this "work of love" and have experienced with Suzanne and our children the process which has made our house a home and our family relationship work.

Oh, we're by no means perfect. But we do try, and we love each other. Spencer W. Kimball once said that we fail only when we fail to keep trying.

This book is full of techniques and methods that represent a consistent, diligent, sustained effort over the years to build our family identity and traditions of cooperation and helpfulness. Suzanne has been an inspiration and example, not only to me, but to our friends, neighbors, and many others with whom she comes in contact.

Suzanne also has a real talent. She's a sponge, gathering all the best ideas available, developing her own approaches, then applying them with *unique* results that make work seem like child's play. To say that she is creative is only a part of the whole. Perhaps her greatest skill is her ability to motivate others by so eloquently convincing them to do better by trying harder. This includes, especially, our children and me. And the hope is, through this book—you.

Michael D. Hansen

Making Home Life Better

No one in the family, especially children, should be excused from the duties that are an important part of home life. By learning early what great joy can come from a task well done, our children are more likely to succeed in today's competitive world. They need to adopt Thomas Edison's attitude, "I never did a day's work in my life—it was all fun." (*Richard Evans' Quote Book:* Salt Lake City, Utah: Publishers Press, 1971, P. 43.)

John Ruskin was even more profound: "If you want knowledge, you must toil for it; if food, you must toil for it; and if pleasure, you must toil for it . . . pleasure comes through toil, and not by self-indulgence and indolence. When one gets to love work, his life is a happy one." (*Evans' Quote Book,* p. 45.)

Over the years, these kinds of thoughts have been running through my head. Since home is where they first become introduced to work, I began searching for ways to teach my children the "joy of toil." It is at home that they will either learn to love responsibility or despise it. I tried to remember what I had enjoyed about my duties as a child. How could I give my children even a better experience?

This mental process began to have its effect. I found that when I was doing a thing that was not my favorite task, I would think of ways to liven up the process and make it more enjoyable and productive. Instead of using all my time and energies in thinking of what my children were not doing to help, I was channeling my thoughts to what they would and could do if properly motivated. The result has been the creation of a fun (and sometimes crazy) assortment of imaginative *games* that make tasks a breeze; exciting *charts* that enhance cooperation; cute *coupons* that do away with "allowances" and usher in "paydays"; and "Happy Helper" *awards* that are earned for jobs well done.

Charting A Course

On a trip, most of us would prefer a good road map to a back-seat driver. You know how irritating it is to be with this type of person when you're behind the wheel. A back-seat driver always seems to remind you of what you aren't doing correctly or which direction you should be going. Finally you get to the point where you are ready to invite that person to rediscover his feet. So it is with children.

Basically our kids want to please us. But how do you think they feel when they're trying, in their child-like way, to do something, and our first reaction is criticism? "Come on, you can do better than that." Next, they do it over until they get it "right." Then, we pull them along by their little hand, telling them exactly what to do, or else. This is not only tough on the kids, but Mom and Dad feel like they need a two-week vacation by the time they get to bed, *every* night.

Once I began making "road maps" (special charts, coupons, games, etc.) for my children to follow that would guide them toward task completion and cooperation, the atmosphere in our home changed. Instead of feeling like a "back-seat driver," I then became a tour guide on a fantastic journey.

Don't take me wrong. There are still plenty of detours and rough roads, but because our family has made a commitment to our "road map," each day brings new excitement and growth. And now, I welcome each morning instead of dreading it.

A road map is a very effective resource, whether it's used for finding Fargo, North Dakota, or guiding the direction of home life. It helps those who use it to understand where they're at, where they need to go, and how to get there. This is the purpose of this book. It's a road map from which you may chart your *own* course. You have my heartfelt wish that your home life will become more fun and productive, and that every member of your family will share the greatest experience on earth—a HAPPIER HOME.

Section One

This is the part of the book you read when
you need a lift and the motivation to change.

It All Starts With You

"It won't work."

"If I don't do it, nobody else will."

"I just can't get my kids to help at home. The only time they do what they're asked is if I lose my temper and threaten World War III; then they grumble, bawl, and generally make life miserable. It's just easier to do it all myself."

Have you ever heard a frustrated parent make such statements—or have you ever made them yourself? If so, join the crowd. But know, too, that things can be different—and better. You simply need to learn a few correct principles, come up with new ideas, and put them to work within the framework of your own family. If you care enough to do that, then success can't be far off.

The Framework

Society, as we envision it, cannot exist without good homes. The home environment nurtures a child's character and shapes his attitudes toward self and others. At home, children learn the difference between excellence and mediocrity. They learn either to work productively or to just "get by." They learn either to be consistent and polished or inconsistent and sloppy. They learn to be in control of their lives—or they learn that it's always someone else's fault.

And who teaches these little children the important

principles of living? Parents do; and their example is the most powerful of all teachers. It follows closely, then, that the very first step in improving your children's attitudes toward the responsibilities and duties of home life (and work in general) is giving your own attitudes a complete check-up—and perhaps even a complete overhaul.

It's no secret that your children watch you constantly. They listen to every word you say, and they imitate you to the tiniest detail. They gravitate toward you because you are the center of their lives. From you they gather strength, approval, and joy. But, with all the gathering, they can also pick up some bad habits. Home is the framework through which children view all aspects of life—and parents create that framework through the power and influence of their own example.

Let's get down to specifics. Mom, there's no doubt that you're the heart of the home. But do you feel a coronary coming on when you try to get your children involved in the responsibilities of home life? Well, consider the possibility that some of *your children's attitudes may very well be reflections of some of your own.* For instance, what do you say when little ears are listening about some of your "favorite" household tasks—like the laundry on Monday morning?

You Find What You Look For

Really, now, how many of us actually love to do dishes, make beds, dust, take out the trash, pull weeds, mow the lawn, do the laundry, and take care of the countless other chores? You may not thoroughly enjoy these tasks yourselves—but you *can* be happy about getting them done, and even have fun doing them. ("No one," after all, someone once said, "has ever injured his eyesight by looking on the bright side of things.") We can also teach our children that such duties are an integral part of home life and must be performed daily. Teaching children to perform these duties is one of the purposes of home life. Your children will view work at home as either a blessing or a heavy burden—according to your example. And they will likewise learn to apply themselves to a task by following your example.

There's an old saying, "How can a mother crab teach her son to walk straight when she herself walks sideways?" And how can you expect your children to enjoy what they're doing when *you* don't enjoy what *you* are doing? The secret of happiness, a wise man once observed, is not in doing what one likes, but in liking what one has to do. We must learn to *like* our many home-centered responsibilities if, in turn, our children are to enjoy and appreciate the work they have to do. If we can accomplish that single goal, the atmosphere of our homes will be like electricity, and the family tradition of cooperation and love will flourish.

A Great Power Source

That word "electric" is an interesting way to describe family life, isn't it? I can promise you that as the attitude in your home improves, there will be energy and enthusiasm to spare. Winnifred C. Jardine, a noted newspaper food columnist and energetic mother and grandmother, has shared with me her idea that fatigue is not caused by a shortage of physical energy. She feels that fatigue is emotionally caused as much as ninety percent of the time.

Frustration, irritation, discouragement, impatience, indecision, and worry are some of the gremlins that invade the mind and burn up energy at a furious rate, robbing time of its work value.

Abraham Lincoln is credited with the observation that a man is about as happy as he makes up his mind to be. I have proven to myself that the best stimulant to energy is happiness in a job.

Do your children know that you can smile? Sadly, what often lingers in little minds are the scowls on our faces because of unpleasant tasks we are called upon to perform, or because the children don't always complete a job the way we want it done. But what do you want your children to remember most about you? I want mine to think I'm the most fun mom in the world. I want them to remember me as a happy person, one who loves being a mom. That's why I try to make housework—and everything we do together—as enjoyable as it can be.

One morning I was enroute to school with a car full of children. I was joking it up with my young passengers recalling my fun-loving college days. But Jenny, my oldest daughter, kept tapping me on the shoulder. I could see that she was trying to tell me something through her eyes, but I didn't get the message. I went on joking and had a wonderful time. Finally Jenny patted me on the shoulder again and whispered, "Mommy, quit it! You're embarrassing me."

Do your children really know how fun you are? Or do they perceive you as the "Big Boss"—the person who tells everyone what to do, or *else*?

Make Memories

Don't be afraid to "let go" and enjoy light-hearted moments with your precious little ones. We are making memories that will last their entire lives.

Margaret Adams, a close, personal friend, was only thirty-five years old when she died of cancer, leaving behind a beloved husband and six precious children. Two years earlier, she had undergone a radical mastectomy, then endured chemotherapy, which caused the loss of her beautiful hair and left her terribly ill. Still, no matter what her trials were, she maintained control of her life and simply refused to complain. Margaret was a great example to me; for, she courageously perceived life from a complete perspective.

One crisp November day, Margaret called, and I could tell something was wrong. "They just detected two tumors," she said, her voice trembling, "one in each of my lungs. But I'm okay now, as long as I hear your bright, cheery voice." And that's just the way she was.

She should have gone to the hospital. Instead, the whole family went to Hawaii—because, as she explained, "We need to make some memories." The trip was cut short when she became desperately ill and required another course of chemotherapy. I visited her; she was very weak and having a difficult time. Still, she didn't talk much about what was happening to her; rather, she smiled and said, "You know, it was such a special time for us in Hawaii. One of the most important things in the whole world to me, Suzanne, is that I leave my family with wonderful memories."

As the weeks passed, I watched death come closer. Yet, still I saw that compassionate, caring light in Margaret's eyes—so concerned about others, never submitting to her own misery, loving to have her little children gathered around her.

I sat at her bedside often, trying to give some of the warmth and light that she had brought to my life so abundantly. Once, toward the last, she struggled to whisper, "Have you gotten pregnant yet?" (We have had a challenge in our home conceiving children as quickly as we would like to, and I had lost a baby a few months earlier.) I said no. Then this frail little woman, wasted to almost nothing by disease and pain, took my hand in hers and said, "Suzanne, when I get to heaven, I'm going to pull some strings, and we're going to get you a baby." I was moved beyond words by her compassion.

When she had gone, I watched those six little children in line beside her casket. Their beloved mother was dressed in white, an orchid placed lovingly in her hands. Her light was in their eyes. The three-year-old cried, "Mommy, come out, Mommy wake up!" Quietly, the other children explained that Mommy had "graduated." "She has gone to Heavenly Father." Margaret had prepared her family well.

The day of Margaret's death, I was cuddling my three-year-old, Julie Ann, and weeping a bit, and she said, "What's wrong, Mommy?" I explained that Margaret had died. Without hesitation, Julie replied, "You know what, Mommy? The angels took her nightgown, and they gave her a white dress, and she doesn't hurt anymore." And I thought, isn't it wonderful to see life through the eyes of a marvelous child.

One day, not long after Margaret's death, I suddenly found myself feeling very discouraged and depressed about my life and negative about myself as an individual. Then I thought of

Margaret, and it seemed I could hear her encouraging me: "Come on, Suzanne. You can do it! Come on, look ahead. You can't change anything you did before, but you can change the future. So look ahead—do the best you can." I knew then that my attitude must change—for myself, for my husband, and for my children. And I made up my mind to succeed. I wanted to build beautiful memories for myself and my family. That's what Margaret would have done.

Mission: Possible

Once we understand the powerful influence of our own attitudes upon the lives of our children, we'll want to examine ourselves minutely to determine whether or not we are reflecting a positive, enthusiastic approach to life and work. Teaching joy through work is possible—it can be very hard and challenging at times, but it will never be impossible if our attitude is right. I'm reminded of a poem dealing with this subject, titled "Don't Quit":

When things go wrong as they sometimes will;
When the road you're treading seems all uphill;
When the funds are low and debts are high,
And you want to smile but you have to sigh;
When care is pressing down on you bit by bit,
Take a rest if you must—but you must not quit.
Life is queer with all its twists and turns
Every which way, as it sometimes will;
And many a person turns about
When they might have won if they stuck it out.
Don't give up, though the pace seems slow;
You may succeed with another blow.
Often the struggler has given up
When he might have captured the victor's cup;
And he learned when the night came down
How close he was to the golden crown.
                        (Source and author unknown)

Success is failure turned inside out. So, when things get challenging and rough, as they sometimes will, look *forward*. You'll find that there are some tremendous challenges; but turn them upside down or backwards, and you'll discover a host of marvelous opportunities for your family. Remember, with the great Justice Oliver Wendell Holmes, that "The great thing in this world is not so much where we stand, as in what direction we are moving."

Your children need—yes, they *deserve*—the kind of example that only you can give, the direction that will point them forward toward success and a happy life. And now, where do they begin? "A child," wrote George Sanderlin, "learns more by imitation than in any other way. Don't we all? And the persons he imitates most blindly and trustingly are bound to be his parents . . . . Nature has made the relationship between parent and child such that beside it any other training bears a certain artificiality."

And it's your attitude, in large measure, that determines the quality of your example. The biblical philosopher was never more insightful than when he wrote, "As a man thinketh in his heart, so is he." (Proverbs 23:7.) We sometimes have little or no control over our physical circumstances, but we most certainly can exercise a great deal of control over the way we view those circumstances and make the best (or worst) of them. Time and again, research, observation, and experience have reinforced the age-old adage:

If you think you are beaten, you are.
If you think you dare not, you don't.
If you'd like to win but think you can't,
It's almost a cinch you won't.
Life's battles don't always go
To the stronger or faster man.
But soon or late the man who wins
Is the one who *thinks* he can.

Remember my friend Margaret? She could do little about the disease that ravaged her body and finally gained its victory over her little portion of mortality. But the ultimate victory, after all, was and is Margaret's, for her example and influence live on. She was pure and forward-looking and never allowed the cruel spectre of death to overshadow her love of life and family. Such love will never die.

Do You Need A Little Help?

I hope we've been convinced that as parents, our own good example is perhaps the greatest resource we have for teaching our children. This is true in all areas of life, from making one's bed in the morning to attending our children's school activities. And, in case you're having difficulty keeping that attitude where it ought to be (on the *positive* side!), I'll devote the next few chapters to helping you make some positive changes.

In the meantime, try getting a head start by completing one little assignment. Before you go to bed tonight, write down one attitude or habit that you are going to change. (It's amazing how simply writing it down will help put it into perspective.) Then tomorrow morning, try getting up with a smile. (No, not a grimace. A genuine *smile*!) Your family might wonder who's coming to visit, but even with all their questions, they'll be smiling too. It's true that a simple smile can help you overcome some of the rough edges of any day.

So . . . keep reading. There's a great experience waiting for you and for those you love—and you have everything to do with it.

"Just remember in the winter, far beneath the bitter snow, lies a seed, that with the sun's love, in the spring, becomes a rose."

Action Follows Belief

Bunker Bean is a novel written in 1912 by Harry Leon Wilson. The book is named after its main character and has become a timeless testimonial to the old saying: "Whatever the mind of man can conceive and believe, it can achieve." In fact, Bunker's belief eventually changed the entire course of his life. (The story of Bunker Bean is retold by Sterling W. Sill in his book *How to Personally Profit from the Laws of Success*, Salt Lake City, Utah: National Institute of Financial Planning, Inc., p. 9-17.)

At first, Bunker wasn't exactly what you'd call a successful individual. Orphaned at a young age, he wandered furtively through life, feeling inferior and afraid of nearly everything and everyone, and ended up living in a cheap boarding-house while working at a low-paying, dead-end job.

One day an interesting thing happened in Bunker Bean's life. He became acquainted with a "spiritualist" who spoke of reincarnation and who offered, in return for Bunker's life's savings and a part of his meager wages, to reveal Bunker's true identity from bygone days.

Taken by the prospect (and also by the spiritualist), Bunker Bean was informed that he had once lived as one of the greatest individuals of all time—Napoleon Bonaparte!

As you might imagine, this "revelation" came as quite a stunning surprise to our timid Mr. Bean. How could he, of all men, ever have been such a stalwart, determined, self-reliant, fearless leader? It seemed beyond the realm of possibility.

Even as Bunker doubted his new friend's words, the shyster was strengthening his position. Life, he explained, progressed in cycles which determined the personality traits of individuals living in a particular time. Napoleon's cycle had been characterized by courage, initiative, and power; Bunker's, in contrast, dictated fear and weakness. But all was not lost, insisted the spiritualist, for just then the cycle was renewing itself. Bunker Bean would soon feel within him the unmistakable stirrings of greatness—of his former self, Napoleon!

As the story goes, Bunker Bean *believed*. Even the thought of who he actually was made him feel different, happier, more powerful. He haunted the library, learned every detail he could about the life and character of Napoleon, hung pictures of the great general around his tiny attic room, and determined to take advantage of his changing life "cycle" and emulate that man to whom nations had paid allegiance.

As Bunker's confidence grew, so did his success. Basking in the reflected glow of an imagined former greatness, he forgot his fears and charged full-speed ahead into the life of an intelligent, courageous, no-nonsense leader. Somewhere along the line his spiritualist friend "revealed" that Bunker had also, centuries before his Napoleon lifetime, lived for eighty-two years as Ramses, one of the greatest of the Egyptian Pharaohs. So Bunker Bean began to believe in the image of himself as both a wise king and an indomitable soldier. Under both mental insignias, he rose rapidly to great wealth and success.

Years later, Bunker learned that he had been the victim of a fraud. The spiritualist had lied to him about Ramses and Napoleon, and Bunker Bean was, after all, only Bunker Bean. But was he? He had cultivated habits of courage, industry, wisdom, and success—habits not easily broken after years of diligent practice. He was now a leader, regardless of his past (or lack of it), and his own self-confidence could now endure, even in the absence of an illustrious family tree. Bunker Bean had truly done it all—because he had *believed*.

Can belief make that big a difference in a person's life? There are scores of examples in history that say it can. But how does a child gain that belief in himself? Is it inborn—or can a loving mother and father help instill it in the child?

To help answer that question, I'd like to share another story, from the book *Charlie's Monument,* by Blaine M. Yorgason (Salt Lake City: Bookcraft, 1976.) Charlie was born with only one arm, and his legs and back were badly deformed and twisted. The people in the town knew Charlie would never make much of himself, and it seemed for a while that they were right. He was still trying to learn how to crawl long after other children were walking and running. When the other children were studying in school, or playing together in the schoolyard, Charlie was sitting alone by his front gate, idly drawing pictures in the dust.

No, Charlie had too great a handicap. Nothing much would ever become of him.

But his mother refused to accept that negative viewpoint. She had a belief in Charlie and in his ultimate potential.

Each day Charlie's mother went out to the pump to get the water for their house—but one day she heard a shout at the door. "Hastily abandoning the weeds in her small vegetable garden, she rushed to the front of the house to find Charlie leaning against the door frame, grinning happily as he drew in great gulps of air. There at his feet stood a pail of water, full almost to the brim.

" 'See, Mom,' he said proudly. 'I carried it all the way and didn't spill a drop.'

Mrs. Langly hugged Charlie to her while she spoke, tears of joy and pride streaming down her face.

" 'You see, Charles? . . . You can do anything you want to if you want to do it badly enough. And you can do it as well or better than anyone else. I knew you could, and now you know it, too.' " (*Charlie's Monument,* p. 16.)

Charlie's life never was easy, even after he learned the power of believing in himself. But he was successful. He was able to reach the goals he set for himself.

Another story perhaps demonstrates this best of all: the story of May and Leslie Lemke. The stories of Charlie and Bunker Bean are excellent allegories of what happens in real life, but the story of Leslie Lemke *is* real life. As is often the case, his true story is stranger than fiction—and more incredible.

Thirty years ago a six-month-old baby was abandoned at the Milwaukee County General Hospital. The officials there didn't know much about the baby except that his name was Leslie—and that he was blind, retarded, and suffering from cerebral palsy. "He was a limp vegetable," the story says, "totally unresponsive to sound or touch." (For the complete account, see "The Miracle of May Lemke's Love," *Reader's Digest*, October 1982, pp. 81-86.)

Hospitals aren't equipped to take care of babies on an ongoing basis, so they made an effort to find a home for the infant. They asked a nurse who lived nearby, named May Lemke, if she would help. "He'll probably die soon anyway," the hospital said.

"If I take him, he certainly will not die," May replied, "and I will take him." She was fifty-two at the time.

Leslie had been fed out of a tube at the hospital; May taught him how to suck from a bottle. She bathed him, cuddled him for hours, talked to him, sang to him. He never moved or uttered a sound.

"Year after year she cared for him, but there was no movement. No smile. No tears. No sound."

May took Leslie out with her, talking all the while. Somehow he would respond. But to what?

For years she tried to teach him to crawl or walk. But the idea didn't sink in. "The Lemkes then had a chain-link fence erected along the side of their property, and May stood Leslie next to it, thrusting his fingers through the openings. After several weeks he finally got the idea of letting the fence support him. He stood. He was 16." Months later he learned to "totter two or three steps."

May never stopped believing in "her boy." She always felt

that something would make a difference in his life, if she just kept working with him.

One day she got the idea of trying to reach him with music. She began to fill the house with music, day after day. She bought an old piano and put it in his bedroom. "Repeatedly, May pushed his fingers against the keys to show him that his fingers could make sounds. He remained totally indifferent.

"It happened in the winter of 1971. May was awakened by the sound of music. It was 3 a.m." She shook her husband awake and asked if he had left the radio on. He said no. "Then where's the music coming from?" she asked.

"She swung out of bed and turned on a living room light. It dimly illuminated Leslie's room. Leslie was at the piano. May saw a smile glowing on his face." He had never gotten out of bed by himself before, never seated himself at the piano, never struck the keys with his fingers by himself. But now he'd done all those things, and he was playing a tune he'd heard before from an album May had played over and over. May Lemke had believed in her boy. And now that belief was bearing fruit.

From that point, Leslie's progress was relatively rapid. He learned to talk, to cry, to use the toilet, to brush his teeth, to give himself a bath, and even to sing with his piano. Leslie Lemke has since begun to join society, to recognize his individuality, his humanness. His mother believed in him and never gave up on him. Her belief has proven to be justified.

What about us, with our children? Few of us have children with serious handicaps. Their potentials are incredibly high. Think of the great things they could achieve if we would only believe in them, helping them to believe in themselves.

Belief is a matter of attitude that can be made a habit. We can develop patterns of action in our lives—habits—that daily show our children we believe in them.

Napoleon Hill, the eminently successful businessman and great philanthropist, believed deeply that we are where we are and what we are because of our daily habits.

He explained that our habits are under our individual

control, and they may be changed at any time by the mere will to change them. This prerogative is the one and only privilege over which the individual has complete control.

The time to start exercising the habit of belief is *now*. Show your children you believe in them. Show them that you know they have powerful innate abilities that are only waiting to be developed. Then follow through by giving them responsibilities around the house, giving them opportunities to become all that you know they can.

Bunker Bean became as wise and powerful as Napoleon, even though he started in the slums, both mentally and physically.

Charlie Langly learned to carry water, to smile, to love, and to serve, even though he was severely crippled.

Leslie Lemke learned to play the piano, to talk, to walk, to take care of himself, even though he was blind, retarded, and suffering from cerebral palsy.

All it took for each of them to succeed was a healthy dose of *belief*.

With that same kind of belief, what could your child become, both now and in the future? Moms and dads have the weighty and wonderful opportunity to help determine the answer to that question.

Getting the Happiness Habit

Understanding the power of example, it doesn't take much imagination to recognize the importance of your own state of mind in providing an environment where children can learn to be happy and productive.

Hence the all-important questions: Are *you* happy? Are your thoughts pleasant a good share of the time? Do you look forward to each new day? Do you wish I would stop asking embarrassing questions? Just remember a favorite saying of mine: "There are times when, if you are not feeling like yourself, it is quite an improvement."

I have learned, through much trial and error, that happiness is a habit which can be acquired by just about anyone who wants it badly enough regardless of circumstance.

Wise old King Solomon made a good point when he observed that "A merry heart doeth good like a medicine, but a broken spirit drieth the bones." (Proverbs 17:22.)

I have heard the poignant story of a powerful, respected monarch who reigned over his country for many years and enjoyed all of the pleasures and prosperity that money could buy. Was he happy? Toward the end of his life he told his subjects that he had fifty years in victory and peace, that he was dreaded by his enemies, and respected by his allies. Riches and honors, power and pleasure, had waited on his call. He had never wanted for any earthly blessing. However, he had diligently numbered the days of pure and genuine happiness, and they amounted to only fourteen.

Two short weeks of happiness is not much to show for a lifetime, is it? And yet the distressed monarch, through his own *right of control*, could have made a significant difference in his life's emotional circumstances.

Bill Marriott, president of the huge and very successful Marriott Hotel Corporation, further emphasized this point: "How do we define the abundant life? Most members of today's society would describe it as having great wealth and material possessions. I can state without hesitation that material wealth has nothing to do with happiness, but is usually the cause of great unhappiness. Happiness comes from the inner peace and spiritual strength we can build up within us, from . . . doing right and from love of family. And it comes from serving and helping others." (Dale Van Atta, "J. Willard Marriott, Jr.," *Ensign*, Vol. 12, No. 10, October 1982, p. 26.)

Most of us are "creatures of habit." We react to petty annoyances and frustrations with grumpiness usually because we've *practiced* reacting that way so long, it has become a habit. The thought comes forcibly to mind that if an individual can so easily habituate himself into a state of *un*happiness, then it certainly should be possible to re-program the mind into an attitude of happiness. Then we, in turn, can bless the lives of our children by teaching them (through our own example) the principles of happy living. That is the way generations of happy parents and children are created. But we must begin here, now, today, to develop this happiness for ourselves.

Psychologists tell us that our self-image and our habits are inseparably connected, and that to alter one is to automatically change the other. In fact, one of the definitions of the word "habit" is actually a garment or an article of clothing. (We're still familiar with the term "riding habit," for example.) So we might picture our habits as the "clothing" worn by our personalities. And, interestingly enough, they fit exactly. In other words, our habits tend to reinforce our self-image, and vice versa. Thus, when we set our mind to changing our old habits and replacing them with better ones, our self-image changes to conform to the new habits. It follows, then, that the better, more positive our habits become, the better we think of ourselves. It's an offer too good to refuse!

Dr. Maxwell Maltz in his popular book *Psycho-Cybernetics* describes a very practical exercise designed to rearrange our habits and point them in a positive direction. Based on the psychological theory that it takes approximately twenty-one days to form a new habit, the exercise calls for a definite commitment to change one's way of thinking for the better. I'd like to quote the entire exercise here, and then challenge you to follow it closely. The results will surprise and delight you!

Practice Exercise

First, say to yourself each morning, "I am beginning the day in a new and better way." Then, consciously decide that throughout the day:

1. I will be as cheerful as possible.
2. I will try to feel and act a little more friendly toward other people.
3. I am going to be a little less critical and a little more tolerant of other people, their faults, failings and mistakes. I will place the best possible interpretation upon their actions.
4. Insofar as possible, I am going to act as if success were inevitable, and I already am the sort of personality I want to be. I will practice 'acting like' and 'feeling like' this new personality.
5. I will not let my own opinion color facts in a pessimistic or negative way.
6. I will practice smiling at least three times during the day. (And one of those times is first thing in the morning—remember?)
7. Regardless of what happens, I will react as calmly and as intelligently as possible.
8. I will ignore completely and close my mind to all

those pessimistic and negative "facts" which I can do nothing to change.

Simple? Yes. But each of the above habitual ways of acting, feeling, thinking does have beneficial and constructive influence on your self-image. Act them out for 21 days. "Experience" them and see if worry, guilt, hostility have not been diminished and if confidence has not been increased. (Dr. Maxwell Maltz, *Psycho-Cybernetics*. New York: Pocket Books, 1971, pp. 109-110.)

You'll notice that Dr. Maltz advises you to say to yourself every morning, "I am beginning the day in a new and better way." This is an example of an *affirmation*—a positive statement which, repeated over and over again, will be accepted by your subconscious mind as truth and will eventually become a reality in your life. Affirmations are wonderful devices, and they can be used to influence your outlook and attitude in a very positive way. You can make the affirmation fit your circumstances, too. If, for example, your patience is running a bit thin, try repeating to yourself ten times (out loud, with whatever feeling you can muster), *"I am patient and loving with my children, and am teaching them to be kind and tolerant with each other."* Repeat this exercise three or four times a day for the prescribed twenty-one days, and I think you'll be astounded at the results. Your children will notice the difference, too!

The following is a list of observations and suggestions for improving your attitude at home:

1. ENJOY THE PRESENT. The philosopher Pascal lamented, "We are never living, but only hoping to live; and, looking forward always to being happy, it is inevitable that we never are so." Somehow we always feel that we'll be happier when the children are in school (or out of school), when we lose ten pounds, when the house is paid for, when we get a better job (or can finally quit our job). But, believe it or not, life will never be free of problems, concerns, and crises. So if we wait until all is well, we'll have a long wait—and happiness will

never come. You have the tools of mind and attitude to become happier, so why not do it now? "If you are to be happy at all, you must be happy—period! not happy 'because of.' " The Apostle Paul shares his feelings, "For I have learned, in whatsoever state I am, therewith to be content." (Phillippians 4:11.)

2. LOOK FORWARD, NOT OVER YOUR SHOULDER. I often recall my friend, Margaret's, words: "Come on, Suzanne. You can do it! Come on, look ahead. You can't change anything you did before, but you can change the future. So look ahead—do the best you can." You can't live successfully in the past any more than you can count on the future to make life better. Like Bunker Bean, be willing to forgive and forget yesterday's fears and faults and inadequacies. It's a truism that you can't change the past. But you can live today so that tomorrow is something to look forward to. A wise man once said, "You must fight for your right to fulfill the opportunity that God gave you to use your life well. You do this when, in your mind, you support yourself instead of undermining yourself."

3. ONE HELPING HAND IS WORTH TWO IN THE POCKETS. If you really want to know what happiness is all about, try going out of your way to provide service to another. Often we get so caught up in our own busy-ness that we fail to respond to the genuine need of a neighbor, a friend, or even a complete stranger. The Savior said, "Or what man is there of you whom if his son ask bread, will he give him a stone?" (Matthew 7:9.)

Service can often be a simple act of compassion. I recall one day as I was pushing a cart down the aisle in a grocery store, shopping with the greatest of ease because my sweet husband was at home tending the children. Suddenly my eyes were drawn to a woman across the aisle from me—a tall, striking woman, very lovely and nicely dressed. It occurred to me that I should speak to her, although we were not acquainted. By the time I had hesitated and then finally made up my mind to do it, she was halfway across the store. I hurriedly made my way through the throngs of shoppers, caught up with her and grabbed her arm. She turned and stared at me as though I had lost my mind. But I took a deep breath, smiled, and said, "Excuse me, you don't know me, but my name is Suzanne Hansen." Haltingly, I then explained to her that I had recently made a New Year's resolution to be more outgoing and complimentary. "I just wanted to tell you how lovely you look, that you're a very striking woman and have a specialness about you." Then, not knowing quite how to close, I wished her a good day and turned to leave. In a second I felt her hand on my arm; tears flowed down her cheeks as she expressed her appreciation for my comments. I had somehow made a difference—and both of us were happier that day because of it. Acts of service can be small or grandiose. But they all produce the same effect: a warm and peaceful feeling around the general area of the heart.

4. BE AS HEALTHY AS YOU CAN. It's a fact that the better you feel physically, the easier it is to have a happy, positive attitude. Of course, it's not always possible to be the picture of radiant health, but the more you can do for yourself in this area, the better. Try treating yourself to well-balanced meals, sufficient rest, and some form of regular exercise. I can guarantee that it will make a big difference in your mental attitude.

Remember, too, to give yourself time to relax, to meditate, to listen to the whisperings of the soul within you, to seek hobbies and activities you can freely enjoy. Happiness comes more readily when you are in tune with yourself.

5. CHOOSE HAPPY THOUGHTS. I have found that even after a day of frustration and challenges, I can always find at least *one* good thing that happened. I try to spend at least a few moments just before bedtime thinking about the happiest moment of my day. Then, no matter what disappointments I've faced, I can still retire with a peaceful feeling—and it's still there when I wake up in the morning, helping to start the day off on a happy note.

I apply the same technique when it comes to my children. I think of each child in turn, and try to remember the thing he or she did that made me the happiest that day. (There are, I must admit, "those days" when I can't think of a single benevolent act on the part of a child. To cope with such emergencies, I concentrate on a special personality trait in that child—sense of humor, neatness, punctuality, etc.—that makes me happy.) My children, too, enjoy a brief bedtime chat when I ask them to tell me about the happiest thing that happened to them that day. This sort of interaction leaves us all feeling warm and friendly toward one another.

6. REMEMBER WHO YOU ARE. It does make life a good deal more meaningful when you know your roots. Keep reminding yourself that you are the wonderful culmination of hundreds of human generations, of your parents' dreams, of God's image and expectations for His children. As a unique individual, you can make of life whatever you desire it to be; you can even change its direction by your own choice. With confidence in yourself and a determination to live joyfully, obstacles are transformed into exciting challenges, and challenges into the fulfillment of your most cherished dreams.

Reaping the Benefits

We've discussed how you can change yourself into a happier, confident, more positive individual. And, if you have even a little desire to make the change, you're headed in the right direction. But I'd like to emphasize the idea that there is an even greater potential here than you might imagine. When parents succeed in changing, their initiative has a domino effect because the lives of their children are profoundly influenced by their actions and commitment. It all goes back to that vital principle of example, doesn't it? Children do, indeed, learn to live by the rhythm of their parents' lives:

"If a child lives with criticism, he learns to condemn;
If a child lives with hostility, he learns to fight;
If a child lives with ridicule, he learns to be shy;
If a child lives with jealousy, he learns to feel guilty.
If a child lives with tolerance, he learns confidence;
If a child lives with praise, he learns to appreciate;

If a child lives with fairness, he learns to be just;
If a child lives with serenity, he learns to have faith;
If a child lives with approval, he learns to like himself;
If a child lives with acceptance and friendship, he learns love in this world today."
(Source and author unknown.)

Genuine, lasting happiness will become a cherished part of life at home as your family grows and improves in many ways through the years. "To go about your work with pleasure," said a very wise philosopher, "to greet others with a word of encouragement, to be happy in the present and confident in the future; this is to have achieved some measure of success in living."

The Attitude of Gratitude

Think back for a moment to the birth of your first child. Do you remember the warmth, the tenderness, the humility, the love with which you welcomed that tiny bundle into your arms? You probably shed a few tears, whispered a prayer of thanks for this new little life entrusted to your keeping. You may have promised to be the best parent this world has ever seen. Most of all, your heart was overflowing with wonder and appreciation for life itself.

Keeping Perspective

How essential it is, amid the rush and clamor of everyday living, to pause occasionally and remember to give appreciation where it is due—to our family, our friends, others who have affected our lives in meaningful ways, and to God, who made it all possible. Such expressions of gratitude are helpful not only in keeping our own lives in proper perspective, but will assist others we touch to live more abundantly, as well.

The story is told of a very successful businessman who, looking back on his life and accomplishments, realized that his early years had been influenced profoundly by a certain teacher. She had retired several years earlier, so he spent some time tracing her whereabouts; then he wrote her a note expressing his appreciation for her influence and example. Her reply went something like this:

"I can't tell you how much your note meant to me. I am in my 80s, living alone in a small room, cooking my own meals, lonely and, like the last leaf of fall, lingering behind. I taught school for 50 years, and yours is the first note of appreciation I have ever received. It cheered me as nothing has in years."

Do you think that gentleman felt rewarded for his efforts and glad that he had taken the time to contact his former teacher? Her reply is a poignant reminder of the need and longing everyone has to be recognized and appreciated. Too often, it seems that painfully few of those longings are ever satisfied.

Before It's Too Late

Perhaps someone you know brings to mind the good woman who worked hard for many years as a faithful, dedicated wife and mother, all with little recognition or appreciation from her family. One evening she said to her husband, "Peter, if I should die, you would spend a large amount of money for flowers, wouldn't you?"

"Of course, Martha," he said. "Why do you ask?"

"I was just thinking," she answered, "that the expensive wreaths would mean very little to me then. But just one little flower from time to time while I am living would mean so much to me."

Why wait until it's too late to give "just one little flower from time to time"?

Count Your Blessings

Lucile Blake learned to count her blessings as the result of a very traumatic experience. In her own words:

I had been living in a whirl: studying the organ at the University of Arizona, conducting a speech clinic in town, and teaching a class in musical appreciation at the Desert Willow Ranch, where I was staying. I was going in for parties, dances, horseback rides under the stars. One morning I collapsed. My heart! "You will have to lie in bed for a year of complete rest," the doctor said. He didn't encourage me to believe I would ever be strong again.

In bed for a year! To be an invalid—perhaps to die! I was terror-stricken! Why did all this have to happen to me? What had I done to deserve it? I wept and wailed. I was bitter and rebellious. But I did go to bed as the doctor advised. A neighbor of mine, Mr. Rudolf, an artist, said to me, "You think now that spending a year in bed will be a tragedy. But it won't be. You will have time to think and get acquainted with yourself. You will make more spiritual growth in these next few months than you have made during all your previous life!"

I became calmer, and tried to develop a new sense of values. I read books of inspiration. One day I heard a radio commentator say: "You can express only what is in your own consciousness." I had heard words like these many times before, but now they reached down inside me and took root. I resolved to think only the thoughts I wanted to live by: thoughts of joy, happiness, health. I forced myself each morning, as soon as I awoke, to go over all the things I had to be grateful for. No pain. A lovely young daughter. My eyesight. My hearing. Lovely music on the radio. Time to read. Good food. Good friends. I was so cheerful and had so many visitors that the doctor put up a sign saying that only one visitor at a time would be allowed in my cabin—and only at certain hours.

Nine years have passed since then, and I now lead a full, active life. I am deeply grateful now for that year I spent in bed. It was the most valuable and the happiest year I spent in Arizona. The habit I formed then of counting my blessings each morning still remains with me. It is one of my most precious possessions. I am ashamed to realize that I never really learned to live until I feared I was going to die. (Og Mandino, *Og Mandino's University of Success.* New York: Bantam Books, 1982, pp. 20-21.)

In our home we have a little game that helps us to remember the many blessings we enjoy from day to day. We call it the "bean-bag game." All family members sit together in a circle. One person has a small bean-bag, and he or she tosses it to another person in the circle. Whoever catches the bean-bag says one thing that he or she is grateful for, then tosses the bag to another person, who does the same. It's a delightful way to spend time together, and we all come away from that game with positive, grateful feelings and deepened love for one another. We all feel better about ourselves, too, because by the time the game is over, each one of us has been named at least once as the object of another family member's gratitude. It's a terrific boost to the spirit to be appreciated—out loud!

How to Develop the Attitude of Gratitude

Sometime soon, you'll want to spend some quiet moments in the congenial company of yourself, just getting to know your blessings and fine-tuning your appreciation. This can best be done by the simple exercise of writing down the things you're grateful for. The list may begin slowly as you try to open up your heart and look deep inside to find the things you genuinely value and appreciate in life. But I can promise you by the time you're through, your "attitude of gratitude" will have deepened and expanded to include many items which might never have occurred to you in the early moments of such an exercise.

Now, with that list in your hand and a more mellow feeling in your heart, you've made a beginning. But don't stop there! The real rewards lie ahead as you make a conscious effort to express this appreciation to those around you—because chances are, they are the ones who need it most.

Appreciative Co-existence

At home, appreciation begins in the closeness of the

husband-wife relationship and flows to other family members. I'm a firm believer in the adage: "The best thing a father can do for his children is to love their mother," and vice versa. Children reared in an atmosphere of courteous, peaceful, appreciative co-existence will likely reflect that graciousness in their own lives, and they'll always remember home as a safe, warm, and secure place to be.

And how about those children? Naturally (well, more naturally on some days than others) you love them, are concerned about their health and well-being, sacrifice for them, want them to grow up to be happy, productive adults. But today, while they are guests in your home, do you take time to really *like* them? Do you enjoy their company as interesting, intelligent human beings of infinite potential? You once spent hours on end studying every movement of your new-born infant; but now that he can walk and talk and dress himself (more or less), is he less interesting? Or have you simply come to take him for granted? If you knew that he would be gone tomorrow, would you spend time with him today? "Do not act as if you had a thousand years to live," warned philosopher Marcus Aurelius. Too often, life goes by before we know it and the important things are left unsaid, the acts of love and compassion—and appreciation—left undone. You may be left, later in life, with an "empty nest," but you need never be left with an empty heart.

Get the Ball Rolling

By now, I hope we can all agree that perhaps the most important ingredient of a happy life is the ability to express appreciation for the large and small amenities of existence. But, you say, that's often easier said than done. Well, perhaps it's a matter of practice—and knowing where to begin. Here are a few simple but tried-and-true ways of expressing appreciation that you might use to get the ball rolling:

Smile—warmly and sincerely. It's not only an ice-breaker, but it lets other folks know that you notice them and feel kindly towards them. (If you've already been practicing this one, as we discussed a few chapters ago, you're definitely headed in the right direction.) A friendly smile communicates instant acceptance, and that's something we all need and value.

Let others know how you depend on them. Whether you say it as a parent, a friend, or a business associate, a sincerely-meant "I don't know what we'd do without you" kind of remark can make someone feel needed, wanted, and appreciated. And when a person—child or adult—feels needed, he works harder and feels better about life.

Give honest, personalized compliments. No matter how young or old they might be, all people thrive on praise and compliments. A tiny baby will react positively to a soft, warm, soothing voice; a 90-year-old great-grandmother still adores compliments on her gorgeous white hair or her terrific grandchildren. And don't feel that you should offer praise only for outstanding accomplishments. Compliment people on everything from their appearance to the orderly way they work. Praise their achievements by writing personal notes.

Listen. One of the best ways you can demonstrate respect and appreciation for another person is by simply listening to what that person has to say. You'll earn his or her undying gratitude—and you might learn something, too. You can stay close to your children—even through those turbulent teenage years—by listening, *really listening*, to what they are trying to tell you. It's not always easy or convenient, but it pays big dividends.

Remember that everyone matters. You'll be making a big mistake if you try to classify people as "very important persons," "important persons," or "unimportant persons." Everyone, whether it's the garbage collector, the company president, or your three-year-old, is important to the wholeness of your life. In the words of a wise man, "Treating someone as second-class never gets you first-class results."

Try to express your appreciation in ways that are most comfortable for you. Ask someone to lunch. Share yourself without being asked. Send a funny card. Buy an unusual gift. Say something nice about someone. Hold a hand. Do a favor.

Lend a book. Phone a friend. Say "thank you."

Obviously, such a list is highly individual and could go on and on. Be creative and have fun with your own style. But in all your doing, remember that those closest to home deserve your attention and appreciation the most. An environment of courtesy and appreciation goes a long way toward building a happy family.

Section Two

They need to know that you care
before they will cooperate.

Getting "Inside" Your Kids

Sure you love your kids. Most parents do; but some are much better than others at communicating that love, because they first get "inside" their kids—they really learn how to understand them.

Eminent family therapist Dr. Elliott D. Landau views the home as "somewhat of a therapeutic community. It is a place where it is safe to grow, where the parents understand the significance of listening, and where the children understand that they have responsibilities and obligations just as their parents do." (Elliott D. Landau, *Today's Family*. Salt Lake City: Deseret Book Co., 1974, p. 88.)

You'll notice that Dr. Landau emphasizes the importance of understanding on the part of *both* parents and children.

Now that you're probably wondering where all this magical understanding might come from—or even what it *is*—let's start by breaking it apart and looking at its components. Quite simply, to understand is to *accept*, to *listen*, to *communicate*, and *to respond with tenderness and compassion*. We'll better understand how to understand as we consider each of these important components in some detail.

Acceptance and More

You will never find a human being on this earth who is the

exact duplicate of another—even in the case of identical twins. Individual differences—physical, intellectual, emotional, spiritual—are the common denominators of our existence. Your responsibility as a parent is to accept your child for what he is, no matter what his gifts or limitations are, and help him to make the most of his potential.

However, acceptance alone is not quite sufficient. Children need to be *cherished*. When children live in a *climate of love*, they feel valued and precious and *special* just because they exist. Then, deep down they can like who they are. Mere acceptance will not build self-esteem.

Parents, please take care to nurture admiration, respect, and love between you and your children. By these actions and by the way you talk, dress, feed, and care for your children, they feel that someone is interested in them, loves them, and *cherishes* them. May your children never question your acceptance.

Lend An Ear

Have you ever had the experience of being listened to but not heard? Unfortunately, children seem to get more than their share of such treatment. A very wise parent once observed:

> How often you hear a little child complain, "You're not *listening*!" And how easily the mother replies, "What do you *want*?" And mostly the child does not really *want* anything, only to communicate.

Someone has said that good listening is not so much the result of using a particular technique as of having a genuine desire to understand. And you can be sure that your own children will sense whether or not you have that desire. But the interesting (and encouraging) thing is that your desire to understand will grow as you discipline yourself to listen attentively and learn to discern the feelings that your children communicate.

Dr. Landau adds some important observations and offers guidelines for those parents who would listen effectively:

First, when a child indicates that he wants to say something to you, and it is appropriate to hear and listen to what he has to say (that is, he hasn't violated some elementary rules of etiquette), stop what you are doing and give him your full attention. If the child is a preschooler, get down to where he is or bring him up to where you are, and then let him talk. By looking right at the child, you encourage him to continue. A child requires the undivided attention of the adults in his world. At all times? Of course not. But when he indicates that he has something to say, and you have indicated that you would be willing to listen to it, then he deserves undivided attention.

Second, with the very young child it might be well to listen with one arm around him so that you form sort of a "cuddle" right then and there. A cuddle is a huddle for folks who haven't football equipment. By doing this you sort of shut out the rest of the world, the family, and the neighborhood, and the two of you are talking with no outside, busy world intervening.

Third, in order to prove that you really are listening, it is important that you answer all questions as they are asked. If it isn't that kind of conversation, then you need to nod often, rephrase what you think you have heard, and then encourage the child to express himself fully. There may even be a time when you will want to try a summation of what you heard. If the world is pressing, learn how to end the conversation with politeness and discretion....

In all children, no matter what age, there is much that they say when they either say nothing or when they say what they do not mean to say. The kind of listening that reads between the lines and that has sensitive antennae up all the time will enable you to hear what is said, especially with adolescents. It will then help you to rephrase what you hear, or interpret, to see if you can focus on what the child may have wished to say but simply couldn't. (*Today's Family,* pp. 101-102.)

And now, Mom and Dad, you might want to give yourself a little check-up quiz to see how you're doing in the listening department. Answer each of the following questions "Never," "Rarely," "Usually," or "Always," and you'll have a pretty good idea of where you stand:

1. Do I look at my children while listening to them?
2. Do I try to understand how my *children* feel instead of thinking about how *I* feel?
3. Do I raise my voice in anger at my children if they interrupt me while I am talking on the phone or visiting with guests?
4. Do I raise my voice in anger at my children when we have disagreements in public?
5. Do I listen patiently to all that my children have to say before I start talking?
6. Am I truly interested in what my children tell me?
7. Do I expect my children to stop what they are doing and listen to me when I need to tell them something?
8. Do I stop what I am doing when my children have something important to tell me?
9. Do I listen in a way that encourages my children to express their real feelings?
10. Do I listen with affection to my children?

Communicate! Communicate!

Without effective communication, we fail to share ourselves—the most precious commodity on God's earth. Then why, you ask, can't we do a better job of it? One has only to glance at the first page or two of a daily newspaper to realize that people of the world aren't generally disposed toward meaningful communication: unless, of course, you define "meaningful" in terms of murder, robbery, artillery, and guerilla warfare.

The solution? "First and above all else," according to Dr. Landau, "A family ought to be a place where it is safe to talk about one's inner space.

"True dialogue means that each party listens *without malice*. Impossible after years of noncommunication? Not necessarily. It isn't easy, but it is possible."

"Real communication," he continues, "means that while we recognize the value of proprieties, every human being has the need to let some inside feelings flow out . . . . in an atmosphere of understanding.

"Communication in a family must be carried on so that the folks involved are physically close to one another during it. A phone call isn't communication. Talking over TV isn't communication. Shouting from one room to another isn't communication. People need to set time aside so that they are eyeball to eyeball when it comes to talking times.

"With children, communicate at the eye level. Get down to them. With adults, don't be more than two feet apart when you say something you really mean. 'Ought to's' can be said anywhere, in any way. Real feelings need to literally be felt and smelled."

Dr. Landau closes his discussion with a word of very positive counsel: "We ought to express appreciation for human acts that we too often take for granted. We ought not to be silent about being appreciative. Appreciation builds human feelings.

"My dad used to tell me that even a dog wags its tail to tell folks how happy it feels to be with them. The least we can do, since we have the power of speech, is to make certain we tell about the good feelings we do have, whenever we have them. Communicating isn't just the process of spewing forth bad feelings. It is also expressing sincerely our appreciation, praise, and feelings of good will and love." (*Today's Family*, pp. 96-97.)

Try A Little Tenderness

Dr. Stephen R. Covey, an expert in organizational behavior and the father of a large family, has written a book titled *Spiritual Roots of Human Relations*. (Salt Lake City,

Utah: Deseret Book Co., 1970.) One of its chapters, "Understand the Tenderness Inside," relates a moving experience from his own family:

My, we had fun together—best fathers' and son' outing yet! Gymnastics, wrestling matches, hotdogs and orangeade, and a movie. The works!

In the middle of the movie my four-year-old, Michael Sean, fell asleep in his seat. His older brother, Stephen (age 6), and I enjoyed the rest of the movie and then I put Sean in my arms, carried him out to the car, and laid him in the back seat. It was cold that night—very cold—so I took off my coat and gently arranged it over and around him.

On arriving home I quickly carried Sean in and tucked him into bed. After Stephen put on his "jammies" and brushed his teeth, I lay down next to him to discuss the night out together.

"How'd you like it, Stephen?"

"Fine," he answered.

"Did you have fun?"

"Yes."

"What did you like most?"

"I don't know. The trampoline, I guess."

"That was quite a thing, wasn't it—doing those somersaults and tricks in the air like that."

Not much response on his part. I found myself making conversation. I wondered why Stephen wouldn't open up more. He usually did when exciting things happened. I was a little disappointed. I sensed something was wrong; he was so quiet on the way home and while getting ready for bed.

Suddenly Stephen turned over on his left side, facing the wall. I wondered why and lifted myself up just enough to see his eyes welling up with tears.

"What's wrong? What is it?"

He turned back, and I could sense he was feeling some embarrassment for the tears and his quivering lips and chin.

"Daddy, if I were cold, would you put your coat around me, too?"

Of all the events of that special night out together, the most important was a little act of kindness, a momentary, unconscious showing of love to his little brother.

What a powerful, personal lesson that experience was to me than and is even now. It has helped explain, to me, at least, why people build defenses and often why communications between people break down.

For Stephen Covey, this incident illustrated some universal lessons:

"*First,* people are very tender, very sensitive inside. I don't believe age or experience makes much difference. Inside, even within the most toughened and calloused exteriors, are the tender feelings and emotions, the heart.

"*Second,* we learn over time how to protect ourselves from getting hurt. We build defenses—sarcasm, cynicism, indifference, aggression, criticalness....

"*Third,* 'toughening our skin' may seem safer, but it may also hinder our growth and keep us apart as individuals." (*Spiritual Roots of Human Relations,* pp. 108-109.)

A parent's special responsibility is to nurture such openness, such tenderness in self and in one's children that such honest, sincere communication will be possible throughout a lifetime. It's quite a challenge to keep the home atmosphere open, trusting, childlike—and vulnerable. But it can be done with constant, loving attention; and it *must* be done if the doors of communication are to remain comfortably ajar.

Acceptance, listening, communication, tenderness and compassion—can you see how they might all fit wonderfully together to form a circle of love in your family? As you weave each one carefully into the tapestry of your own life, new dimensions of caring and understanding will open to your view. Generations will be blessed by your efforts.

Dads Do Make A Difference

It was natural for me, as I pondered this chapter and its importance to the book, to turn to my husband, Michael, for help. Mike has been at this job of parenting as long as I have, and he's a constant source of support and strength to me. He takes his role as a dad very seriously, and I've seen him both struggle and grow in it.

As we talked, we concluded that he should write this chapter. That would give us the father's viewpoint and would allow Mike to talk with other fathers, heart-to-heart. Here, then, is the father who makes such a difference at our house:

Like many fathers, I enjoy sports. Football is my favorite, and that preference has been picked up by my son, John. As we watch TV games together, I've noticed that Johnny watches me as much as he does the game. He sees me get excited about a play and jump right up off the sofa and cheer. When I first did that, John's eyes grew wide as he watched. But the next time I did it, he was right there with me, jumping up and cheering.

Johnny tells me that someday he's going to be a great quarterback. He's noticed that I place a lot of importance on the quarterback position. If something's important to Dad, he wants to be part of it.

One day we bought a little Nerf football and went out into

the yard to try it out. He dropped back to make a pass as I streaked across the yard, and he hit me right on the button. "Great pass, Johnny," I would say, or "What a spiral!" Then his eyes would light up and that smile would nearly reach from ear to ear.

Johnny will probably grow out of wanting to be a quarterback. That won't matter a bit. What's important is that we're building a relationship with one another. We're learning how to have fun together; and I'm showing my son that he's an important person in my life. My daughters know that they're important to me, also. They really look forward to our "dates" or just sitting and talking or doing anything together.

Build the Relationship First

All of this fits right in with what Suzanne has been talking about in the rest of this book. The father plays an important role in getting kids to want to do their part at home (and be happy about it!) Dad is a catalyst. When he's involved things start to happen. And the place for the father to start is with his relationship with his children.

Think of the people you know. Some are simple acquaintances, and even though you'd be happy to help them out when they're in dire need, most of the time you don't concern yourself with their necessities. But your close friends, the people you really love, are a different matter. You watch out for them; you keep alert to their problems and needs.

The same principle applies to relationships in the home. If the home relationships are cool or strained, people often become selfish, more concerned with their own needs than with anyone else's. But when the relationships are close and loving, a whole different mood prevails. Each person wants to please his fellow family members. With that kind of attitude, household duties become home joys.

The most important suggestion I have about the role of the father, then, is this: *Build a strong and loving relationship with each of your children.* If you have that, everything else will follow.

The HOW of Building Relationships

Most of us know how to build good relationships. But sometimes we overlook vital elements. Let me review some things I've tried and others have shared with me:

Spend time with each of your children. Children thrive on attention—that's why they often act up when they aren't getting enough.

Picture two children. The first gets plenty of time with her father. The second finds her father is always too busy to do much with her. Which child do you think feels more secure in the home? And which do you think will be more willing to respond to the things her father asks of her?

It's not always easy to find time for our children, even when we recognize they're among the very most important things in our lives. I've found that one of the hardest things in my own life isn't going to work every day—it's coming home and being a good father, doing all the things I know I should be doing. And at the top of the list of what we all need to do is spend time with our children.

But all we need to do is change our attitudes. It takes much less energy to put your feet up and read a newspaper or watch TV at the end of a long day, but it brings greater and lasting results to spend time with a child!

Talk with your children. Some parents can go for *days* without saying much of anything to their children. The effects of such a life-style may not be immediately apparent, but they'll eventually show up in the child's behavior.

One father took a look at his life and decided he needed to talk with his children more. So he put it on his business calendar. Every Monday night, between 7:30 and 8:00 he had a private interview with one of his children. Since he had four children, that meant a good heart-to-heart talk with each one of them at least once a month.

At first it was awkward to sit and talk with his kids—he just wasn't used to communicating with them. But as the weeks passed it became easier and easier. And now both he and the children look forward to their monthly visits.

Incidentally, that one talk a month has benefits that carry over throughout the month. When the children have something they want to share—whether it's a problem or something exciting in their lives—they feel comfortable in going to Dad about it.

Play with your children. Kids love to play—that's one of their main interests in life. When an adult enters that realm, the adult instantly endears himself to the child.

Think of the times you play with your kids: teasing, tickling, laughing, playing a board game, playing tag, playing horsey—those are some of the funnest times for both you and the kids! The kids remember those times together; and the bonds between you grow stronger and stronger.

Go on dates with your children. Mom and Dad should go on dates together regularly—once a week certainly isn't too often. But what about the kids? Would they enjoy going on a date with Mom or Dad? The answer, of course, is yes!

Suzanne and I try to go on dates regularly. The kids notice, and they want to be a part of it. "Why don't we ever get to go on a date?" they asked. We decided the kids were asking a legitimate question. Why couldn't they go out with us, too?

We're probably as busy as anyone else, so it wasn't easy to find time for something else. But we love our kids, and we wanted them to know it. So I sit down with them each month and work up a schedule. Suzanne and I rotate, so at least once a month each child gets a date with either Mom or Dad. The kids love it. We don't do expensive things together. We buy ice cream cones or see bargain movies or go window shopping or roller skating. It hasn't really mattered what we did. Each child was alone, one-on-one with Mom or Dad. That was *neat* to them!

These dates have been great for our family. They help Suzanne and me grow closer to each of the children, and it helps the children feel more loved and special than ever before.

Learn effective, loving discipline. The child doesn't exist who doesn't sometimes need to be disciplined. But how a parent administers that discipline makes all the difference in the parent-child relationship. A parent can punish in ways that damage the relationship; or he can discipline in ways that will build both the child and the relationship.

The key is to discipline in love. The raised voice rarely communicates love—but a parent can communicate disapproval without yelling. Withholding love can be devastating to a child—but sending the child to a time-out room can be very effective.

How do *you* discipline? Does your child know you love him even when he's been naughty? Or does he feel rejected and unworthy? If our children understand that we love them unconditionally, despite their failings and weaknesses, we'll go a long way toward drawing them ever closer to us. In the end, we'll probably get farther if we view ourselves as motivators rather than disciplinarians.

Invest in Your Child

Here's the bottom line of what I've been talking about. If you build a sound relationship with your child, you'll be taking the best step you possibly could. You'll be creating patterns in your lives where love and service and selflessness are part of your very being. And those kinds of attributes will automatically result in children who will happily help at home.

These attitudes are like the techniques of a skilled gardener. Anyone can plant a seed, water it, let the sun shine on it—and end up with a grown plant at the end of the season. But it takes an expert gardener to come up with a healthy, strong, and vital plant. The wise gardener knows when to water, when and where to prune the plant back, how to resist garden pests, and a score of other important tricks.

The same applies to parents. Anyone can give birth to a child, feed it, and enable it to grow to adult size. But it takes someone who is willing to invest extra time and effort to rear that child to be a *responsible, thoughtful* adult.

Building Disciple Families

An excellent editorial from *Time* magazine underscores

these ideas. The editorial was written in 1967; it's probably even more relevant in our day:

> To a startling degree, American parents have handed child raising to educational institutions that cannot or will not do the job. More than one-half of U.S. mothers work at least part time. And some fathers hardly see the kids all week. According to psychiatric social worker Virginia Satir, the average family dinner lasts ten to twenty minutes. Some families spend as little as ten minutes a week together.
>
> Studies show that father absence has baneful effects (especially on boys) ranging from low self-esteem to hunger for immediate gratification and susceptibility to group influence. Hippies of the late '60s and early '70s commonly fled from father-absent homes in which despairing mothers either overindulged their children or overpressured them.
>
> 'Discipline comes from being a disciple,' says psychoanalyst Bruno Bettelheim; both words come from the Latin word for pupil. Children become the disciples of parents who enjoy and back up one another, and whose mutual respect and ungrudging praise for work well done makes children draw a positive picture of themselves. But the approach must be genuine. The young mind is quick to spot the phony.
>
> In disciple families, 'no' is said as lovingly as 'yes.' The children learn to wait. The parents refuse to buy them this or that until they prove themselves mature enough to use it wisely. Allowances are given not as a dole but to train children in budgeting necessary expenses. Little girls are not pushed into premature dating. The parents couldn't care less that 'everybody else do it.'
>
> One way to help build a disciple family is to make sure that parents and children never stop doing meaningful things together. Family games with

father involved, hikes, building projects, and political debates—such activities underline adult skills that children then naturally want to have. Just because evening meals get tense is no reason to quit them. There is no better ritual for spotting and curing the tensions....

Many 80-hour-a-week executives might try something else: rejoining their families. In recasting themselves as fathers, they might recast their values and change their lives. Making a living is important, but selling more soap should not destroy the process of raising sons and daughters. (J. Allan Petersen. *The Marriage Affair.* Wheaton, Illinois: Tyndale House Publishers, 1971, pp. 137-140.)

The Next Step

Okay, fathers, we've committed ourselves to build our relationships with our kids. That's the best thing we can do, but it isn't everything. Here are a few things we can do to help our kids cooperate in the duties of home life:

Set an example. When kids have a father who works hard *at home*, and enjoys his work, the kids are more apt to learn to love work. But don't miss those words I highlighted there: the children need to see the father at work. It's not enough that he puts in fourteen-hour days at the office. He needs to work around the house as well, and the children need to see him doing it—and enjoying it.

Here's a poem that supports the idea of the need for example. The poem is entitled "Show Me."

I'd rather see a sermon than hear one any day;
I'd rather you would walk with me than merely show the way.
The eye's a better pupil and more willing than the ear;
Fine counsel is confusing, but the example's always clear.
Best of all the preachers are the men who live

their creeds,
For to see the good in action is what everybody needs.
I soon can learn to do it if you'll let me see it done.
I can see your hands in action, but your tongue too fast may run.
And the lectures you deliver may be very fine and true.
But I'd rather get my lessons observing what you do.
For I may not understand you and the high advice you give,
But there is no misunderstanding how you act and how you live.
(Source and author unknown)

Work with your kids. When the house needs to be cleaned, when the dishes need to be washed, when clothes need to be laundered, Dads can join in and help. By working happily with the kids, Dads can show that work can be fun. And the parents and the kids can have fun in working *together.*

Support your wife. One wise man once said, "The best thing a father can possibly do for his children is to love their mother." Show your kids that you love their mom—and that you support her in what she's trying to do. As your wife tries to implement these ideas, join with her in her efforts. Learn about the approaches and ideas. Learn how they work. And be as one with your wife in making those ideas work in your own situation.

Jesus once spoke about the importance of a husband and wife being as one:

He which made them at the beginning made them male and female, and said, For this cause shall a man leave father and mother, and shall cleave to his wife: and they twain shall be one flesh. Wherefore they are no more twain, but one flesh. (Matthew 19: 4-6.)

The more we can unite with our wives in all things, including our approaches and techniques of child rearing, the happier and more effective we'll be.

Use the approaches yourself. Every father has work he's responsible for around the house. He's often the one who's in charge of repairs, mowing the lawn, raking the leaves, tending the garden, shoveling snow off the walk, washing the car, and on and on. I speak from experience when I say it's a great delight to have your children help on such tasks. (Sometimes they're more hindrance than help, but it's great to have them around!)

When you're doing your work, why not involve your kids with you? And do it by using the same techniques your wife is using in the house. That way, with a united front and an allied approach, you and your wife will be teaching the children both ways!

Give rewards to your children. Kids are like anyone else: they're more willing to do things they're rewarded for. That's part of what this book is about: helping you to give rewards to your children for the things they do, making their work more interesting and enjoyable.

Rewards come in many forms: verbal thanks and praise, physical touch, emotional sharing and empathetic feeling, material giving. The most powerful rewards are the ones that most fulfill the needs of the child, and those would generally be the emotional rewards. But don't be confused—emotional rewards can be implicit in all other kinds of rewards!

When your children do well, reward them for it. Give them a kiss or an accomplishment coupon, a batch of pennies or a bit of praise. If you're able to give them what they need and want, they'll be more willing and able to give you what you need and want.

Our Responsibility—and Opportunity

Fathers can have a great impact on the feeling in the home. They can often make the difference between success and failure with the children. And fatherhood is our most important task in life. Harold B. Lee said, "The most important work you ever do will be within the four walls of your own home."

David O. McKay expressed a similar thought: "No other success can compensate for failure in the home."

It's an important job, and many of us come to it with little or no training. Life trains us for many things: for driving a car, for making our way through school, for our occupations. But we don't really get any training for fatherhood. We often have to muddle our way through and do the best we can.

But our situation isn't anything new. Parenting has been this way throughout history. As Jay Allen Peterson, the founder and president of Family Concern, Inc., said:

> When has childrearing been easy? At what time in history has the negative portion been dormant? Without minimizing the pressures of our time, we must recall that each age has its own peculiar hazards and anxieties. It has always been tough to rear unselfish and responsible children. We should realize, as someone has said, that it probably takes more endurance, more patience, more intelligence, more healthy emotion to raise a happy human being than to be an atomic physicist, politician, or psychiatrist. (Previously cited, *The Marriage Affair*, p. 5.)

Nearly every home has several things in common: a mother, children, and work to be done. And there's one other element that can make a lot of difference: a father. The father can be the catalyst that makes everything else work. He's the one who, by word and example and attitude, can make everyone else's life a whole lot nicer.

It's a great responsibility and challenge. It's also a wonderful opportunity!

Raising "I Can" Kids

When I was just about to get married, my mother sat down with me for a heart-to-heart talk. "Everything won't be easy for Michael and you," she said. "But things will run more smoothly if you'll remember just this one thing: you can catch more bees with honey than you can with vinegar."

I've found that's also true of raising and teaching children. You'll have much more success with children if you use a kind approach, positively reinforcing the good things they do.

Your children aren't all you want them to be, and they are by no means all they want to be at this point in their lives. But if *you believe* they can succeed, they'll believe it, too. That attitude can be projected by your actions, your facial expressions, your verbal expressions, and your tone of voice.

Children believe in themselves as much as you believe in them. You are a mirror; you reflect to them what they are.

What happens when a child believes in himself? Suddenly he has the power to do all sorts of wonderful things. Moms and Dads, do you wish your kids would help around the house more? Teach them to be "I can!" kids, and not only will they be more willing, but they'll become more able. You'll be amazed—and very pleased—at the difference you see in them.

This is the process of building self-esteem—and high self-esteem can do more to help a child succeed than just about anything else.

How can we build high self-esteem in our children? How can we teach them the "I can!" approach to life? Childrearing experts are a great help here. I've seen the truth of their counsel in my own family.

Tip 1: Help your child by investing in him.

A great student of human nature, Sterling W. Sill, once wrote about how we get out of life just what we put into it. "There is a basic, fundamental law upon which all of the others rest," he wrote. "called the law of the harvest, it says that 'as a man soweth so shall he also reap.' "

What Mr. Sill is saying is that we get out of life exactly what we put into it. And the same is true of our relationships with our children.

> If you want someone to punch you on the nose, you don't need to make a formal request or argue or reason with him about it. The quickest and most certain method of getting this response is simply to punch him on the nose. If you want someone to send you a Christmas card, all you need to do is to send him a Christmas card.... If you want someone to like you, all you have to do is to like him. If you want him to trust you, trust him. We are all human magnets. Our deeds, our attitudes and even our thoughts attract in kind. If you frown at someone, he scowls back at you. If you want smiles, give smiles. You can know in advance how everybody will react to a given situation. Therefore, a great power is placed in your hands if you choose to use it. Just figure out what you want, and then give accordingly. (Sterling W. Sill, *Leadership*. Salt Lake City: Bookcraft, 1950, pp. 15-17.)

I really believe in Sterling Sill's philosophy. The law of the harvest works with children just the same as with anything else in life.

Children are like cakes or buildings or TV or anything we make or build. They are just as good as the materials we put into them. If you put in time, love, and patience, you'll get quality children in return.

Time is one of the key elements. The more time I spend with my children, the more I learn about them, and the more my love grows for each one. Time is one of the most valuable gifts we can ever give to our children. By giving a child of our time, we're saying, "You're important to me. I'm busy with a lot of concerns, but you're more important to me than anything else."

"I can!" is planted like any other seed. We, the parents, plant the seed in our children, then nurse it with tender loving care. In doing so, we bring into force the natural law of the harvest. If you plant and nurture a seed of wheat in the ground, you get valuable sheaves when it's time to harvest. If you plant and nurture a seed of self-esteem in a child, he'll enjoy a high level of self-esteem throughout his entire life.

Tip 2: Help your child by showing you support her.

In their excellent book, *101 Ways to Boost Your Child's Self-Esteem*, Dr. Alvin H. Price and Jay A. Parry describe the importance of support:

> Every child inevitably grows older! That statement is more profound than it may at first appear, because as a child grows up, his needs for support change. When your child's world expands, you'll find that she needs support in her new activities and the new aspects of her life. (New York: American Baby Books, 1982, p. 52.)

Every one of us has seen the truth of that. Do you remember your child's first steps—how unsure and wobbly he seemed to be at first? Remember how you had to coax him to get up and keep trying again and again? Your encouragement was important. But now remember how much easier it was for him when your arms were stretched out to him. Your support made a lot of difference. Then he could somehow muster the courage to try still one more time.

Your support eventually led to success. Think of that

special, rewarding experience you shared when the child finally succeeded and walked for the first time. Can you remember those eyes, that special smile of joy? He had a challenge, and you helped him face it. That support made a lot of difference. It helped him know you care; it helped him know you'll always be there with your arm outstretched to encourage and help him when he's down.

No matter what age our children are, or what stage they're going through, they constantly need to feel the outstretched arm, the feeling of approval that comes from loving and supportive parents, knowing the parent is there to support his efforts does much to help a child grow in his self-esteem.

Tip 3: Help your child learn how to deal with the fear of failure.

Fear of failure can prevent children from even trying. But if parents can help their children face that fear, and deal with it constructively, the child will be able to grow.

In *Your Child's Self-Esteem* by Dorothy Corkille Briggs, we find the following:

> All growth involves uncertainty. 'What will it be like?' 'Will it be dangerous?' 'Will there be trouble if I do it?' Movement toward the unknown can turn on anxiety. The child who feels safe to retreat needs far less courage to venture because he hasn't burned his bridges behind.
>
> The option of retreat without dishonor makes any child more likely to embrace the unknown. (Garden City, New York: Doubleday and Company, 1970, p. 115.)

When parents ask their children to do a new task, it's not uncommon for the children to respond, "I can't do it." They're afraid of not doing it right, or they're afraid the parents will be displeased.

Here's a great opportunity to help a child grow and at the same time to build his self-esteem. If you can help the child to succeed at the new task, you've built his self-esteem and helped him see it wasn't so hard after all.

At the same time, though, the child may genuinely not be ready for the new task. You may want the child to learn to tie his shoes—but his fingers just won't work that way yet. In that case, allow him to retreat. He can try again another day, another week. But in the meantime, you've shown him that you respect him enough to let him grow at his own pace. The result: his self-esteem grows, and eventually he'll end up being more capable.

Tip 4: Help your child by avoiding negative labels.

Positive labels give a child something good to shoot for. Negative labels give a child something bad to live up to. I've found in talking to my children that they respond much better and grow much stronger if I talk positively.

Here's what the experts say about labels:

From Briggs: "The labeling words—adjectives and nouns that describe a person—are the ones that cause trouble. Words like 'dawdler,' 'messy,' 'procrastinator,' 'sloppy,' 'rude,' 'mean,' 'selfish,' 'naughty,' 'nice,' 'good,' 'bad,' 'shameful,' and so on are judgmental by nature. Such labels have no place in the vocabulary of nurturing adults." (*Your Child's Self-Esteem*, p. 86.)

From Price and Parry: "Negative labels destroy self-esteem, and too often the child begins to believe them." (*101 Ways to Boost Your Child's Self-Esteem*, p. 89.)

I feel very strongly about labels. When I was in the fourth grade, I became very ill and missed a lot of school. When the school year ended, my mom and the principal had a little meeting. "Suzanne may want to stay back in school and repeat the fourth grade next year," the principal said. "She's missed a lot of material. But it's up to her. She's a smart girl, and whatever she decides will be okay."

I thought it over and decided to take the fourth grade over again. I didn't want to proceed through school without the material I'd missed.

But that decision opened me to a lot of grief. The other

kids suddenly labeled me as a dumb-dumb, someone who couldn't cut it with normal kids. They acted like I had a second-class brain—and figured I should be treated accordingly.

Then a very sad thing began to happen: I began to believe my classmates. It wasn't long before I stopped progressing in my studies. By the time I got to fifth grade, my teacher and my mom met in a parent-teacher consultation, and my teacher said, "I don't think you should worry about Suzanne not doing well in school. That's just the way she is, and she'll never do well. Why don't we concentrate in art—that's one thing she can do well."

Children look to us for their identity. It's vitally important that we give them positive labels. We can help them see themselves as "I can!" kids, rather than "I can't!"

I'm living proof that labels can help as well as hinder. Finally, with loving parents and some help from friends, I was able to come out of my mental doldrums and be viewed as a first-class person again!

Tip 5: Help your child learn the importance of perseverance.

"Perseverance is a quality that builds self-esteem," say Price and Parry. "The more a child perseveres, the more success she'll achieve. And success leads directly to heightened self-esteem.

"When a child gives in to discouragement or fatigue, she suffers a loss of self-respect. Sometimes it's best to leave a job and return to it later, but it can be damaging to anyone to start a job and then give up on it indefinitely." (*101 Ways to Boost Your Child's Self-Esteem*, p. 31.)

I had a hair-raising experience that showed me how important perseverance is. My son, Johnny, had received a bright orange sting-ray bike for Christmas. He was a little small for the bike, and he needed help getting on and off, but he wanted desperately to learn how to ride. My husband went out one morning and worked and worked with John. Every time Mike would let go of the back of John's bike, John would fall head-first onto the road. As Mike went running to Johnny to pick him up, Johnny always said the same thing: "I'll never learn how to ride a bike."

But he kept on trying. His eyes filled with tears from being hurt and from being disappointed at not learning—but still he tried. You could see in his face that he felt like a failure. "I'll never be able to ride this dumb bike," he muttered, over and over.

Mike didn't agree. "Sure you can, John. Just keep it up, and before you know it you'll be an old pro."

Finally John had had enough. He kicked the wheel of his bike and said, "I'm never going to ride a bike as long as I live," he shouted, and he huffed into the house.

We all had lunch. Then Mike said, "Come on, Big J. Let's try one more time." Johnny hesitated for a minute, but then silently nodded and went out the door with his dad.

The next thing I knew, Johnny was riding his bike back and forth in front of our house. The bike was so wobbly that it looked like it would fall at any moment. Johnny looked at me with a giant grin. "I can do it!" he yelled. "I can do it!"

"I knew you could!" I yelled back. Then he started down the slope near our house. "Johnny! Do you know how to put on the brakes?"

He got the funniest look on his face, and I knew he didn't know how to stop his bike. Then he just grinned and shouted, "No! But I can always jump off!"

I thought my heart would stop several times that day. How I wished we had gotten him a three-wheeler. But as I look back on that day, I can see in my mind a little blond-haired, blue-eyed boy with success written all over him. He had persevered in the face of obstacles, and he had come out on top. His self-esteem soared. And his continued success went right up with it.

That night when I tucked him into bed, he looked up at me with those big eyes, and he whispered, "Did you see me, Mom? I can ride all by myself!"

"I saw you," I replied. "I knew you could do it!"

Tip 6: Help your child by letting him be self-reliant.

It was hard to stand back and let Johnny get hurt over and over again as he learned to ride that bike. I would have preferred to step in and help him. But I've learned that self-reliance helps build self-esteem. And self-esteem, of course, leads to greater success.

I took Johnny roller skating for the first time. He was on his bottom more than he was on his feet—but there was a determination in his face I'll never forget. He knew that if he paid the price he would be successful. Each time he would hit that hard floor, the pain on his face was as difficult for me to take as it was for him.

Finally I decided to step in and help him out. "Let me skate by you and hold your hand," I said. "Maybe you can learn better."

"No, Mom," Johnny answered. "I have to learn by myself."

By the time we left two hours later, Johnny was up more than he was down. He was sore for a week after that, but that didn't matter. He had ventured out on his own, and he'd been successful. He was becoming an "I can!" kid.

Tip 7: Help your child learn the value of patience in the face of difficulty.

My eight-year-old, Jenny, learned a lot about patience through an ordeal that demanded a lot of her.

When she first began to have severe stomach pains, we rushed her to the hospital, fearing she had appendicitis. They diagnosed her problem as stomach flu. She cried all through the first night. The next day we took her to the hospital again. And again, they said it was stomach flu.

Poor little Jenny couldn't relax or sleep. She stopped eating. Finally it was more than we all could bear, and we insisted the hospital try to do more. Doctor after doctor examined her, but no one knew exactly what was ailing her. Day after day I sat by her hospital bed, cradling her in my arms and trying to comfort her. They couldn't do anything to help her with the pain until they knew precisely what her problem was.

Then one day they noticed that large black and blue spots were appearing on her legs, and her feet were swollen much larger than normal size. These were the clues they'd been looking for. They knew what Jenny's problem was. She had a very rare blood disorder that caused her capillaries to hemorrhage, internally.

But diagnosing a problem isn't the same as treating it. Even though the doctors were able to define what Jenny had, they said that medical science didn't know how to treat it. They assured us it wasn't fatal, sent us home with pain medicine and instructions on how to care for her until the problem went away.

By the end of the week, Jenny's lower extremities were completely covered with the bruise-like spots. She was so uncomfortable she couldn't even communicate with us. She lost over ten pounds, an incredible amount for a young child, and we were fearful of losing her, despite the doctors' assurances.

Her condition continued for weeks. The adhesions on her skin would go away; then they'd reappear in a few days. Sometimes it was pure will-power that got us through the day. Jenny would say, "I'll never walk again. I'll never be able to play again."

"No, honey," I'd answer her. "This disease will eventually go away. That's what the doctors told us." I prayed they were right.

The weeks seemed to pass so slowly. Finally, after what seemed forever, Jenny started to regain her health.

Jenny showed great courage throughout her ordeal. She also learned an important lesson: if we are patient, things usually turn out for the better. She also learned that life doesn't always give us what we would wish. But when we have the "I can!" attitude, we're able to deal better with whatever comes our way.

Tip 8: Help your child by showing he is truly loved, unconditionally.

Outside the doors of home, the world is always critical. It can find plenty of things wrong with us and with our children. But things don't have to be that way in the home. We can control the atmosphere in our home to make it a sphere of joy, a place of love where our children can reach their full potential.

The world is generally conditional. They like children if they do this or that, if they have this particular brand of shoes or that particular style of clothes. But that's not how it should be in the home. We need to let our children know we love them no matter what they do or what they're like. Certainly we prefer some behaviors over others, but a child needs to know that you love him even when he doesn't measure up. In the end, that's what helps a child become an "I can!" kid: he knows that you love him without conditions.

I can't tell you the number of times my children have "driven me crazy" with some of the stunts they've pulled. But I do love them, and I try to constantly show them. In the end, I think that's the most valuable thing any of us can do: love our children unconditionally, and show it lavishly! If we can accomplish that task, we've accomplished everything. And our "I can!" kids will succeed throughout their lives.

Section Three

Here's the "How To."

Incentives Make Things Happen

Motivating children to work is a fascinating challenge. Working isn't something that comes naturally (at least it doesn't to me or my children), so you can't just sit back and "let it happen"—unless you want to wait for a very, very long time. The value of good, hard, honest work is one of the most important concepts you can teach in your home, for it will serve as a solid foundation of discipline on which your children can build good character and habits of industry and success. The learning begins with your example—and your willingness to create an atmosphere of fun and enthusiasm along the way.

I have found from personal experience that one of the most effective ways to motivate children is by providing incentives for good behavior and helpfulness. Until a child is old enough and mature enough to generate his own incentives (or simply to do something because he knows it's right or should be done), he needs the motivation of some type of reward to keep him interested and willing to perform tasks that must be done as his part in helping the home and family to run smoothly. And the more enthusiastic and creative you are about providing the rewards, the more anxious your children will be to earn them.

You may find that you'll need quite a variety of incentives to match the different needs and personalities of your individual children. It will take some time and experimentation to discover which kinds of incentives appeal to each child; but, once you've solved the "puzzle," you'll know just how to proceed.

We'll talk about a number of incentives in this chapter. Don't feel obligated to try every one of these ideas (mothers can only work twenty-six hours a day, after all), but choose one or two and adapt them to the needs of your own family. By then, your mind will be bubbling over with wonderful new ideas suited especially to your own children and circumstances.

Adding the Trim

Have you ever made a dress, or seen one in the store, that was rather plain and uninteresting? If you're like me, once that dress was finished or home from the store, you immediately started visualizing ways to make it more exciting, attractive, unusual. By adding a bit of colorful trim here, a shiny button there, a cluster of brightly embroidered flowers somewhere else, you turned that dress into an original, one to be worn often and with delight.

Like the added decorations on that dress, incentives for children make their work more appealing, help them to get excited about performing many different kinds of tasks, and add fun and interest to their day.

What child wouldn't react positively to these incentives? "After you've done your practicing, you can come with me for a ride to the store." "When the toys are all picked up and in place, we'll have a super story time." "When the garden is weeded, we'll have a water fight, or we'll run through the sprinklers."

If you choose rewards carefully, they can accomplish a dual purpose. When you say to your child, "Finish raking the leaves, then come in and you can help me whip up a batch of cookies," you're not only offering a tasty incentive, but that son or daughter will be gaining some valuable skills in the areas of cooperation ("You grease the cookie sheet while I finish mixing up the dough."), mathematics (How many teaspoons are in a tablespoon?), and cooking principles ("No, dear, the cookies won't bake if we don't turn on the oven."). Your trip to the store can also be a learning experience—in fact, almost any reward can be not only fun, but educational.

I might add just one word of caution about these verbally-promised rewards. Remember that consistency is *absolutely essential* when it comes to fulfilling your end of the bargain. Whether you're handing out rewards or disciplinary action, a child *must know* that you mean what you say. If you promise a walk in the park upon completion of a certain chore, be sure you can keep that promise—or don't make it. And don't say "maybe." Your child simply won't hear the word when you say, "Pick up your room, and *maybe* we'll go for a ride," and he'll feel betrayed if you don't come through with the reward.

Whatever incentive you offer, try to make it one that you will enjoy, too. You can't always do that; but generally an activity is more fun if one of you isn't gritting your teeth. Besides, if the reward is something that you can both look forward to, you're more likely to get *your* work done, too!

Just for Starters

The possibilities for motivational tools are endless, and many excellent ideas will be products of your own imagination. Here are a few that have been effective with my children; I'm sure you'll be able to think of many others, but these will make a good beginning.

1. **Hand Puppets.** There are many different types of hand puppets, and most are simple to make and use. For example, you can buy a furry dust-mopping glove at the store, then add a pair of "googly" eyes, and you've got an "Oscar the Grouch" to help your child dust. (Of course, the puppet actually does the dusting, and the child merely helps, right? Such an approach makes dusting a lot more fun—I'll guarantee it!)

Do you have old socks around your house that have long ago lost their mates? If your house is anything like mine, you can really "sock" it to the kids with sock puppets! Use your imagination, and let them help. You can add felt eyes, yarn hair, decorate with marking pens, or almost anything that strikes your (or their) fancy. Before you know it (and depending on how many stray socks grace your laundry room), your children will each have several pet puppets to help them pick up toys, dust, and do other chores that are more fun to do with a friend.

Kids can decorate a paper-bag puppet with just about anything from crayons to glued-on ric-rac; they even talk, if you work the flap just right. They're not as durable as sock puppets (or those made of fake fur or other fabric), but they're great fun and very good at picking up toys. They come in a variety of sizes, too, which makes for some interesting creations.

Naming your puppets makes the whole idea even more fun and personal. Donny Duster and Percy Pick-up will know just what their respective assignments are, and they'll become favorites with the children. I'll bet, too, that the youngsters will come up with some wonderful names on their own.

2. Pretend. Children are naturally creative, and most of them love to make believe. Mine enjoy pretending that they are puppets on strings; Mom is the "puppet master" and pulls the strings as each child does a specified task. Or Mom could "wind up" a puppet with an imaginary key; the child goes to pick up a toy or other item, then returns to Mom to be "rewound."

In a game called "What am I?", each child pretends to be a certain animal as we work in the house. At the end of the work time, we all come together in a circle and guess what sorts of animals have been loose in the house that day. We've had elephants, giraffes, dogs, cats, and various other creatures as workers in our home. The most interesting one we had was a snake, played by our inventive son John. We watched him slither and slide through his chores; it took him a bit longer than the others, but he did a good job and it was lots of fun.

A very similar game is "Guess What I Am," where a child can improvise a truck, a plane, an animal, or just about anything he sets his mind to. It's exciting for a child to "be" something as he is busily engaged in his work, because the time flies by and an old job is completed in a new and different way. After all, wouldn't an airplane pick up a toy differently than a turtle?

3. **Sing-Along.** If your children are like mine, by the time they have lived a few years they have developed quite a repertoire of favorite songs—everything from those catchy "Sesame Street" tunes to the songs with sweet, simple messages they learn in Sunday School. Most youngsters love to sing, usually at the top of their lungs; and I've found that energetic work and whole-hearted vocalizing go well together. Wasn't it our old friend Mary Poppins who said (or rather *sang*), "a spoonful of sugar makes the medicine go down"? Try singing with your children as you work together; let them teach you some of their favorites, and share with them some of your own to make everyone's work go faster and easier. Or play a lively record or tape and move to its beat as you watch one task after another almost do itself. Music not only calms the "savage beast"; it can also brighten up what might otherwise be a very ordinary day. (After the jobs are done, by the way, you might want to put on some very restful, relaxing music, lie down on the floor together, close your eyes, and think pleasant, kindly thoughts for a few minutes. You'll be surprised at how friendly you all feel toward one another after such an interlude.)

4. **Color Fun.** Dye the tips of several toothpicks with food coloring, each one a different color. Then, holding the toothpicks in your hand so the colors are concealed, have each child pick one. The child who picks the red toothpick, for example, would then pick up every item in the house that was red and out of place, and put that item in its proper location. The child who picks the blue toothpick would do the same with blue-colored objects in the house, and so on. If for some reason a child feels he's been unfairly burdened (if, for example, he picks green and there happen to be three dozen

green objects out of place that day), you might adjust the timing so that different toothpicks are chosen every fifteen minutes (or whatever seems fair).

5. **The Great Bean Give-Away.** Each child is given about thirty beans at the beginning of the week; they are stored in individual jars (I use baby food jars) with the child's name on them (adding a bit of flare, of course—like our daughter's "Jolly Jenny Jar"). As the days go by, whenever one child picks up an out-of-place object belonging to another child, the child who owns the object must give a bean to the child who picked it up. The child who has collected the most beans by the end of the week is the winner and receives a special prize.

At Easter time, this game works especially well when you use jelly beans in place of the usual dried navy or kidney beans. Because jelly beans are easy on the sweet tooth, they provide an even greater incentive to win. At week's end, the victor has a jar full of delicious treats, *plus* the "Jolly Jelly Bean Award."

6. **Pick-A-Peanut.** Here's one all the nuts (or squirrels) in your family will especially enjoy. To each of several peanuts, glue or tape a small sign with one or two key words on it that indicate a job to be done; i.e., "bed" (for making your bed), "hair" (comb your hair), etc. Then hide the peanuts in each child's room. As each peanut is discovered, the child reads the key word and does the job.

A variation on this theme is to play "squirrel." My daughter Jenny, for example, likes to pretend she's a squirrel or a chipmunk. We decorate a paper bag as "Jenny's Tree" and put it in a special location. Then Jenny starts to "gather" her nuts for the winter. She finds one peanut, reads the key word, stashes the nut in her "tree," does the job, then continues the process until all the nuts are safely gathered. (Even much younger children can play this game if you use drawings instead of key words—and hide the peanuts in slightly more obvious places.)

7. **Sticker-Up.** Chances are, your friendly neighborhood variety store stocks an almost endless supply of motivational tools in the form of bright, colorful, many-shaped stickers. There are arrows, stars, hearts, animal shapes, smiley faces, even "well done," "excellent," and "champ" stickers. Take your children to the store with you, and let them pick which ones they'd like to work for. You can use stickers as rewards for work completed, for learning that difficult piano piece, for being kind to sister or brother, or for helping Mom or Dad without being asked. More often than not, a sticker is its own reward; but you also might want to consider having a little race to see who can get the longest line of stickers by week's end, with a special prize for the winner.

8. **Charts and Posters.** Anything that will get a child's attention is a step in the right direction, and certainly a chart or poster that will motivate him toward good thoughts or behavior is well worth the time you spend putting it together.

There are so many different types of posters and charts, and so many ways of creating them, that I've reserved a chapter later in this book to share in detail some of my ideas on this important subject. But let me assure you here that with just a little bit of effort and imagination, you can provide your family with an unending variety of delight and motivation that will pay great dividends, both today and in the future. Use charts and posters to celebrate a season or a special holiday, to work toward a goal, to record tasks completed, or simply to brighten an otherwise ordinary day. Children love to see visual portrayals of themselves and their surroundings, and most of them enjoy keeping track of what is going on in their lives from day to day. Charts and posters can be simple or elaborate, Mom-made or kid-created. The important thing is that they reflect a spirit of happiness and enthusiasm in the home.

As an example, one day while the other children were at school, Julie and I sat down and made a poster. We thought one with bees would be a nice touch; so we drew a beehive, a few little bees flitting around it, and I wrote on the poster,

"I'm a busy bee all day, whether I'm at work or play." We attached three small packages wrapped with yellow paper; the idea was that as the children completed their household jobs on time (and without reminders) for two weeks, they could pick one of those "sweet treats" off the hives.

As we walked the others home from school, Julie insisted excitedly, "There's bees in our room, there's bees in our room!" A little uneasy about the idea of a bee in their bedroom, the children said to me, "Did you get it out, Mom?"—to which I responded, giggling, "No, it's a happy bee." They asked, "How can you have a happy bee? Doesn't it sting you if it's happy or not?" I smiled mysteriously and said, "Oh, you'll see." Well, when they arrived home to find the bee poster on their door, you can imagine that they were excited and anxious to earn their special treats. And it certainly added a note of intrigue to what could have been a very ordinary school-day homecoming.

Holidays and special seasons lend themselves naturally to colorful posters and charts. January is a time of new beginnings; February, the month of love; March, a month-long green-and-white celebration, complete with "kindness kites"; July, a time for special feelings of patriotism; and the ideas go on and on.

9. **Leverage.** There are (as I'm sure you realize) certain kinds of motivation that are prompted by a sense of expediency. In other words, if a child fails to perform an expected task or duty, he is allowed to reap the consequences of his choice. For example, if house rules say that the children don't eat breakfast until their beds are made, you can safely assume that not too many beds will go unmade. By the same token, if they get dressed before breakfast, you'll find that it takes them about half an hour; after breakfast, it may stretch to three or four hours. (No, friends, that isn't child abuse. It's *incentive*!) Such motivation, used with wisdom and kindness but firmly applied, can prove effective in some of family life's most challenging circumstances. And, as with most reward systems, consistency is the key to making them effective.

Games That Make Household Responsibilities More Fun

Playing games and having fun while doing housework is just a way of getting everyone to enjoy what they usually dislike doing. I find that housework or anything else in life is just about as fun as you make it. A dress may be plain until you add frilly lace. A Christmas tree is just a tree unless you trim it. In the same respect, a job is just a job unless you make it interesting, enjoyable, and rewarding.

Usually things seem harder than they really are. All we have to do is get started. Games and other fun activities can be used to help children enjoy what they have to do until the children establish good work habits for themselves. It's like Mary Poppins said in the delightful movie, "For every job that must be done, there is an element of fun. Find the fun, and snap, the job's a game." She also said, "Every task you undertake becomes a piece of cake, a lark, a spree, it's very plain to see that a spoonful of sugar makes the medicine go down."

Special Games

Tic-Tac-Toe. Very easy to use and apply in your home. This is how it works: Get a large piece of poster board. Draw a tic-tac-toe game just as you would normally, but on a large scale.

In the top row of spaces write: make bed, brush teeth, comb hair. In the middle row write: sweep kitchen, get dressed, pick up ten things. And in the bottom row write: practice piano 20 minutes, vacuum one room, help with dishes. Cut out colored circles to place over each job as it is completed. (I like putting a smiley face on the disc.) Each child has his own playing card, so jobs can be changed depending on the age and stage of the children. To the child, as long as everyone has the same number of squares and jobs, Mom is fair. The winner of the game is the first one to yell, "Tic-tac-toe!" when there's a blackout (all jobs done and covered). Then the winner gets to wear a special smiley face for that day.

Toss a Task. This is also played on a playing board as in the previous example. The game is very simple. In each square is a picture (for the very young ones) or words that indicate a task that a child needs to do. A button or penny or some flat object, even a small rock or a lid, can be thrown onto the card. Wherever it lands, that job is to be done. If it lands on a square that has already been done, then the child tosses again until all the tasks have been completed. I find that at the end of the game all children find great satisfaction in their accomplishments.

Adaptations. If the child tosses his marker on a square and it indicates, for example, a shirt or sock, that indicates to the child that he should dress in that item. Or picture a whole outfit in one square. The child runs and gets dressed, then returns to the playing card. The first few times it might be helpful for Mother to help out, but the child can and will be able to do it himself if he is shown several times. If a child seems to be slow, challenge him to try to do one square by the time a song ends or by the time you finish whistling a tune. This will help prevent nagging.

Tickety-Time. Children don't always understand how time flies by. If you think back, you might remember when you were small yourself, and how time could drag on forever. Remember how long your school days were? Did you ever watch the clock? To a child, it seems like there's all the time in the world. They don't see time race like grown-ups do. Here's a game that has helped my children understand how to use time. It's easy to do and very helpful.

Out of a piece of poster board cut a square about 12" × 12". Write at the very bottom: "Tickety-Time, I'm a Happy Helper." On the 12" × 12" paper, put a large plate face-down and trace a circle. In the middle of the circle draw eyes and a nose. Attach hands on the nose with a brad so that the hands move around the clock. On small cards write the tasks that need to be done, such as: make bed, get dressed, comb hair, wash face, eat breakfast, help with dishes, brush teeth, pick up toys, put clothes away, empty garbage cans, set table for lunch or dinner, brush teeth (at different times of the day), night-night, and sleep tight. By each item or picture drawn on the card, write the time the task is to be done. For example, on card #1 you might write: "I can make my bed at 8:00 a.m." On the bottom of the card draw a little clock face which indicates 8 o'clock. When the child completes the job, he goes to the large clock and moves its hands to the time indicated on the job card—little hand on the eight, large hand on the twelve. As they pick a card with a task on it, they look at the numbers, and then they can move the hands of the clock to the time shown. This helps children become familiar with the clock and some of the times that certain things need to be done.

Sounds Like. This is another game that makes housework fun. It is a guessing game. You say a word that sounds like a key word related to a certain job. Examples: "Ted" sounds like "bed"; "best" sounds like "dressed"; "share" sounds like "hair"; "rush" sounds like "brush"; "wishes" sounds like "dishes," and so on.

It's interesting to teach children the key words. For instance, "teeth" means brush your teeth, "toy" means put toys away, "room" means straighten your room, "wash" means wash face and hands, "pet" means feed the pets. Give the child the clue, let him guess until he guesses the task, then he completes the job and returns for a new clue. Mother can do this while she is doing jobs of her own. Have the sheet of paper in your pocket with the name of the clue or the word which is the clue and what the clue means. This helps children become more familiar with different words that sound like other words.

With small children, you can go over words that sound alike; then, when you say that first word, they in turn try to remember the matching word. For instance, while you're driving, use the key word plus the clue word and children can fix it in their memories. By teaching these words you can also broaden your young child's word capability and understanding. There will be immediate response, for example, when you sweetly say the word "joy." Your child will know right away that it's time to pick up a toy.

Phonics. Let's call this game "Fun with Phonics." Here we introduce a certain letter and words that start with that letter—the letter "f," for instance:
1. I put my shoes on my _____. Circle the correct picture or word:
         five   four   fork   feet

   (The correct answer is, I put my shoes on my *feet*.)
2. I like to eat my _____. Circle one of the following pictures:
         fan   fox   flag   food

   (I like to eat my *food*.)

Other examples:
3. I make my _____ every morning.
         bear   bead   bat   bed

   (I make my *bed* every morning.)
4. We like to clean our _____.
       horse   hand   hole   hunger   house

   (We like to clean our *house*.)
5. I always put my _____ away after I play with them.
       tuba   table   tiger   ten   turtle   top   toys

   (I always put my *toys* away after I play with them.)
6. I remember to brush my _____.
         toad   tow   tree   toe   tack   teeth

   (I remember to brush my *teeth*.)

7. I always wash my _____.
   fairy   fruit   four   fox   fish   face
   (I always wash my *face*.)
8. After meals I help with the _____.
   dog   deer   doll   doctor   duck   dishes
   (After meals I help with the *dishes*.)
9. I like to help my mom _____ the floors.
   valentine   vest   vase   vacuum   violin
   (I like to help my mom *vacuum* the floors.)
10. Every night I put my _____ on before going to bed.
    pig   pumpkin   pear   parrot   pajamas
    (Every night I put my *pajamas* on before going to bed.)
11. When I help at home, it makes me feel _____.
    horse   house   hurt   hop   happy
    (When I help at home, it makes me feel *happy*.)
12. It makes my mother _____ when everyone pitches in and helps.
    milk   marbles   mirror   mitten   merry
    (It makes my mother *merry* when everyone pitches in and helps.)

Use your imagination. You'll be surprised at the fun you discover.

Joke Jar. First, brightly decorate an empty pickle or mayonnaise jar and label it "Joke Jar." Then fill it with folded pieces of paper with jokes written on them. Next, give every child a list of jobs. On this list should be all sorts of jobs, depending on the age and stage of your child. Examples: make bed, get dressed, comb hair, wash face, put clothes away, set table for breakfast, brush teeth, practice piano, empty garbage cans, dust one room, vacuum one room, feed the fish, feed the dog, feed the cat, etc.

After each job is completed, the child runs to the kitchen, puts his hand into the joke jar, and pulls out one joke and reads it aloud. It's fun to see the response when everyone hears the crazy joke.

Continue to collect new, clean jokes that the children can

share with friends. It's great to hear everyone laughing and having fun together. Time flies by quickly, and each person learns to have fun while doing something to help out.

Examples of jokes and riddles that can be used:
What kind of house weighs very little? A lighthouse.
When is a store so much like a boat? When it has sails.
When are two roads unpleasant? When they are crossroads.
What ring is the very best for a telephone? Answering.
What did the big chimney say to the very small chimney? You're not big enough to smoke.
Why would a spider make a good baseball player? Because it is good at catching flies.
If a carrot and a cabbage run a big race, which would win? The cabbage, because it's ahead.
How do you make a slow horse faster? Stop feeding him and make him fast.
Why should you never try to sweep out a room? Because it's too big a job. Just sweep out the dirt and leave the room there.
What kind of a bird helps you eat faster? A swallow.
What kind of dog has no tail? A hot dog.
What always has an eye open but never sees? A needle.
Why is a baseball team like a pancake? Because its success depends on the batter.
What gets wetter the more it dries? A towel.
Why does an Indian wear a feather head-dress? To keep his wigwam (wig warm).
Why shouldn't one trust the ocean completely? There's something fishy about it.
When are boys like bears? When they go barefooted.
On which side does a leopard have more spots? On the outside.
If athletes get athlete's foot, what do astronauts get? Mistletoe.
What bird is the heaviest? The crane.
Why do bees hum? Because they don't know the words to the song.

Why is Santa Claus the best gardener in the world? Because he loves to ho, ho, ho.

What kind of socks does Santa Claus wear? Panty ho ho hose.

What fruit kept best on Noah's ark? The preserved pairs.

Why was the elephant the last animal on the ark? It took him such a long time to pack his trunk.

Where did Noah strike the first nail? On the head.

When the flood waters went down, was Noah the first one out of the ark? No, he came forth.

Where was Solomon's temple? On the side of his head.

What did Goliath think when David hit him with a stone? Nothing like that had ever entered his head before.

What was the phone number in the Garden of Eden? Adam 8-1-2.

Who is the best doctor mentioned in the Bible? Job, because he had the most patience.

Try to remember the jokes you used as a child and add these to your "Joke Jar." It's good, "clean" fun, and it makes work easier. One of the most corny oldies I can remember: "What's 20 stories high and yellow? Empire Banana."

Pick a Stick. This is fun and also very easy to play. Save popsicle sticks, or use "tongue depressors." Get approximately thirteen of them. On each one, write (in black felt tip pen) a job the child needs to do. The child sits on the floor with the sticks face down in front of him, or they are tossed onto the floor in front of him. Then the child picks one stick at a time, does the job and returns, puts the stick he has completed into a box or a jar, then picks another. When the sticks are all returned to the container, the child is done. It is a wonderful feeling to be "done." Most parents never have that "done" feeling (although they might occasionally feel "done *in*"!). But children also need to have time to be children after all the work is done. Kids, after all, are only kids once in their life. Ten years a kid, fifty years an adult.

Look and Remember. This game is a fun way of teaching children to remember. On each of four 8" × 10" cards, draw or write three pictures or words representing jobs to be completed. The cards are shown to the child one at a time. The first card is shown for approximately two minutes, then placed face down on a table or the floor. The child tries to remember all three jobs on the card and do them without coming back for a peek. When one card and all its jobs have been completed, he goes on to the next card until all four cards are completed. Then he's free to do something that he would like to do.

Example: Card #1—three pictures are indicated on this card for three specific jobs: make bed, get dressed, wash face. It seems simple; but for some children, remembering three items to do is quite an accomplishment.

Card #2: wash face, comb hair, big smile.

Card #3: set table, vacuum one room, dust one room.

Card #4: practice the piano, pick up the things in your bedroom, empty garbage cans.

You can add whatever jobs you'd like. For older children, write key words for them to remember. As you play this game, you could make it progressively more challenging by adding one or two more pictures or words to each card to see if they can recall extra tasks. This reinforces in the child's mind what his responsibilities are around the house. It also helps answer the question, "What do I have to do?" because tasks can be "programmed" into the child like any school subject. I feel that it's just as important to teach your children good habits as it is to teach them the "three *r*'s." This particular game helps our children start to use their memories, too. And if a child has good work habits and can remember, he will have what it takes to achieve good grades in school and be successful in work and society.

Jolly Jelly Bean Jar. This game was mentioned in a previous chapter, but I'd like to explain it in detail. It's a fun, interesting game and creates excitement in the family. Each child should have his own jar, whether it's an empty small peanut butter jar or a baby food jar. It is fun to let each child decorate a label or a piece of paper that could be glued to the front of the jar. Have them write their name (or you can do so) in plain sight so he or she can read it easily and each child knows which jar is his. Then give each child thirty jelly beans in his jar.

Before officially starting this game, it's essential that you establish some guidelines and rules. Explain that Mother will have a list near her at all times—a kind of "tally sheet." When a child finds an article that is out of place and belongs to a brother or sister, he will privately show it to Mother and secretly return it to the place where it belongs. Then Mother writes a mark on the tally sheet next to that child's name. (This "secrecy" rule prevents any child from provoking another child by taunting, "Nanny-nanny-nanny, I've got your toy," or something of that sort. So the children don't compete against one another; rather, they're competing against themselves.)

At dinnertime, the jelly bean jars are placed around the table. The person whose items were picked up by other family members must "pay" one jelly bean for each item of his that was found out of place. Mother, tally sheet in hand, directs the "payments"—and if the child complains, he loses an additional jelly bean. This helps everyone remember not to leave their things out of place. At the end of the week or the time allotted, everyone gets to keep their jolly jelly bean jar. So you can believe that everyone wants to be careful not to leave their things around. It's also fun to include Mom and Dad in this game; you'll start becoming aware of your own habits as well as those of your children. The game doesn't take much time or effort to put together—but it does take some effort when it comes to changing one's habits.

Easter Egg Hunt. This is a fun, exciting game that can be used any time of year, but is most appropriate around Easter time.

At any variety store you can find a package of small plastic eggs. Bring them home, take them apart, and put "clues" inside each one. You can write out "make your bed," or you can just use the clue "bed." Then hide the eggs around in different rooms and send the children on an egg hunt. Carrying an

Easter basket, they find one egg, open it up, read the clue, complete that job, put the egg in their basket, and go on to search for the next egg. The jobs should be done thoroughly, as you have explained before the game starts. It's also fun to put pieces of gum, lifesavers, pennies, balloons, and other tiny surprises inside the eggs, which add to the excitement and fun.

A similar game uses paper eggs with clues written or drawn on them; these can also be hung or hidden in various rooms of the house. Each child has a different color of egg—Jenny is yellow, Johnny is blue, Julie is pink, Lynette is green—so the child knows that he is only to find the eggs that are his color. (As reminders, you might want to tie colored ribbons loosely around the children's necks. Then they hop like bunny rabbits to do their jobs. It adds flair to the game and makes it fun for the children. It's interesting, too, to watch them laugh and giggle as they willingly complete those tasks that seem so challenging to other children.)

More Fun Games

Here are some additional games and activities that you might wish to adapt to the needs and interests of your family.

Treasure Hunt. There are many different types of treasure hunts that you can use in your home to make things lively. Some are games in which you give clues to help the children understand which jobs are to be done first. I find that giving specific jobs, one at a time, helps children to feel equal to the tasks and not overwhelmed. Sometimes children have a hard time when you give them three or four things to do; but if you give a child one thing at a time, it becomes simpler.

The treasure hunt does just that. One clue is given, the child performs the task, then he finds another clue after he finishes that job. For instance, at the foot of the bed one morning you can lay a pirate's knife. On the knife is a piece of gum, saying, "To a sharp boy, make your bed." This clue helps the child remember, without nagging, that he needs to make his bed as soon as he gets up. The next clue can be hidden near the bottom of the bed, this one a clue to "get dressed." After he gets dressed, he might find another clue in the pocket of his clothes: "Wash face—comb hair." The child is given just one clue at a time, so he feels like he's climbing the stairs not eight or ten at a time, but one at a time. And climbing stairs isn't as hard as you think when it's only one step at a time.

I remember traveling to Mexico and visiting many large,

Mayan ruins with hundreds of steps leading up to their entrances. I recall looking up at one such edifice and thinking, "I will *never* get up to the top!" But I found that taking one step at a time was much easier than thinking of hundreds of steps at once. So it is with children—they need to think of only one step at a time.

As the child completes each job on the treasure hunt, it would be added fun for you to give him a round piece of paper resembling a gold doubloon. Each time he completes a job well, he can collect a gold doubloon, and he can use these tokens at the end of the week to purchase something from your family store, or buy a pirate ship at the store or a boat that floats in the tub. This helps a child see, in essence, what he does every day and how the rewards add up. Have you ever noticed how washing clothes or doing the dishes every night gets a little challenging? Well, if you add up how many times you do the dishes in a year, you'll understand why it becomes quite challenging for you to keep doing it with a smile. By the same token, it's hard for a child to be enthusiastic about the same tasks every day. But by counting those gold doubloons, he'll see how many things he has really accomplished in a week. It will boost his self-esteem and make him feel better about life in general. Too often, we human beings look at what we have to do instead of at what we have actually done. It's important that we help our children see the best in themselves by telling them, "Look at what you have done," "Look at what you can do," and "Look at how you're doing it so well." This will help our children feel better about their responsibilities.

Sometimes a child feels that his mother can never stop giving him jobs. As we've stated before, a child is only a child once—so give him opportunities to explore and do things that he'd like to do. It's wonderful for children to help in the home, but it gets challenging for a child when he can't see the end of the road. Work can be like an interminable journey to a child; but if he can see the end in sight, it's easier for the child to cope and makes him more eager to help around the house. So it's important that we set a goal. When a child has completed a particular assignment, then he may do something he enjoys.

And now, back to our treasure hunt. Make up clues that would lead each child to find the jobs that need to be done. At the end of the hunt, you might leave a chocolate-covered coin in the bottom drawer of the child's dresser. Or you could have a small but brightly-wrapped gift hidden somewhere in his room at week's end. This makes life really exciting. (You can find 10¢-15¢ items that are most appropriate—pencil sharpeners, gum, barrettes, lifesavers, school folders, homemade treats, homemade stuffed animals, etc.)

Here's a sample treasure hunt that you might want to adapt to your own uses:

First, an introductory clue, written on a piece of paper folded like old parchment and burned around the edges: "Let's cast off for new adventures on the high seas of life, and while we do so we'll help our home become ship-shape. So just follow me bloomin' treasure map."

Clue #1: "Mate, follow me instructions. Take five large steps to your bedroom, and be sure to leave it as a true sailor would—ship-shape."

Clue #2: "Take six steps to your drawers, get your clothes on, and put those P.J.s away."

Clue #3: "Take sixteen tiny baby steps and find where the bathroom is. Then comb your hair, matey, and wash your bloomin' face."

Clue #4: "Take ten middle size steps to the kitchen and help set the breakfast table for chow. We pirates love our grub!"

Clue #5: "Take twenty steps and help clear off the table in case a furious storm hits the seven seas."

Clue #6: "Sixteen steps to get to the piano and practice."

Clue #7: "Ten steps to the vacuum—then vacuum one room, matey."

Clue #8: "Take twelve large steps, eight small steps, and dust one room."

Clue #9: "Five leaps, six tiny steps to empty the garbage

cans."

Clue #10: "Ahoy, matey! You have just about reached the treasure. Turn around three times and say, 'Yo, ho, ho, and a bottle of pop. I'm a good helper, and I'm not going to stop!' Take fifteen large pirate steps, and go look in the bottom of your drawer."

In the drawer is the prized doubloon, which might be chocolate covered candy. At the end of the week, if a child has collected eight wrappers and glued them up on a chart, or collected the candies and put them in a jar, then next time they go for the clue at the bottom of the drawer it would be the brightly-wrapped gift or some other surprise. (Little girls might enjoy beads that are strung or beads to string, or some other small gift.)

Holiday Incentives. Many different games can be designed to go along with holiday themes, and you can plan ahead for such occasions. During the Halloween season it's fun to dress up in old sheets and pillowcases and to make ghostly sounds as you complete assigned tasks. It really adds to the fun of the Halloween holiday—and we feel like we're "catching the spirit," so to speak.

Links of Love. This game is a fine one to be played at Christmas time. Each child has twelve pieces of paper (approximately the width of a ruler, 6-8 inches long), each with a job written on it. One at a time, those pieces of paper are given to the child, who reads the word or looks at the picture and identifies a job that must be done. Then, every time a child completes one of the tasks willingly, he may add that link to the family "love chain." At the end of working time each day, the children add their links to the chain. It takes everyone working together to make the chain as long as it should be, and it helps everyone to see the importance of cooperation. The chain could start in the kitchen, draping from room to room along the ceiling line, and the children will soon see how fast the love chain can grow. Working together builds unity and love within the home, and every time you look at the chain it's very rewarding. You might use one color per child, or you can mix and match colors and let each child pick what color he would like to use each day.

Another activity for the Christmas season is to place a number of little reindeer around the home. Each one carries a loving message ("These deer are just a little remin*deer* for my sweet dears.") and a job to do ("To my dear Johnny, thank you for being such a dear when it comes to helping me out; it helps me so much when you make your bed."). When each reindeer has been gathered up and the jobs on it have been completed, the child is finished.

Guessing Games. "Guess What I Am" is a lively game. It can be played in several different ways. For example, each child can make believe he or she is a certain type of animal, as suggested in an earlier chapter. Members of your family can use their imaginations when it comes to playing this game.

Another enjoyable guessing game is to describe a task or something to be used in completing a task. When a child can guess what the task is, he whispers it in your ear, and if you nod your head "yes," then he runs to get it done. If the guess is incorrect, then he may guess again and again until he guesses correctly. When he finishes the job, he may come back to you for another clue to help him guess another task. Besides getting the work done, this game can help the children learn to listen carefully—even children need to learn how to listen.

Remember Where. This game uses thirty cards that match (fifteen pairs). All cards, which contain pictures of jobs to be done, are placed face down on the floor or table, and the child chooses a card. He continues choosing until he finds the matching card, then runs to complete that task. The process is then repeated with new cards. Example: When a child chooses a picture of a bed, he then turns over the cards on the table (they are made of 3" × 5" cards or other pieces of construction paper or poster board) until he finds the matching bed. He turns them both face up, then runs to complete the task of making his bed. When he has completed the task, he takes those two matched cards and sets them aside. This makes a fun game and helps a child learn to identify objects. A hair brush, toothbrush, clothes, dishes and glasses—there are all types of symbols that you can use on these cards to help your children be excited about memorizing those jobs that are important for them to do.

Pick-n-Try-It. Begin this game by folding a piece of paper in several sections. (You'll remember this hand-worked puppet-toy as the "cootie" game you played in grade school.) On the outside of the toy, its sections are numbered from one to eight; inside, the panels are also numbered. Under each inside flap is a job to be done—make bed, practice piano, put clothes away, etc.

In order to play the game, each child has one of these paper toys and must work it for his brother or sister—which means that some cooperation is involved. A child picks one of the outside numbers, and his brother or sister moves the toy a corresponding number of times and opens it to reveal the inside numbers. The child doing the choosing then picks one of these numbers, and the flap is lifted to reveal a task to be completed. Imagine your children having fun with this little game, getting their jobs done, and cooperating at the same time!

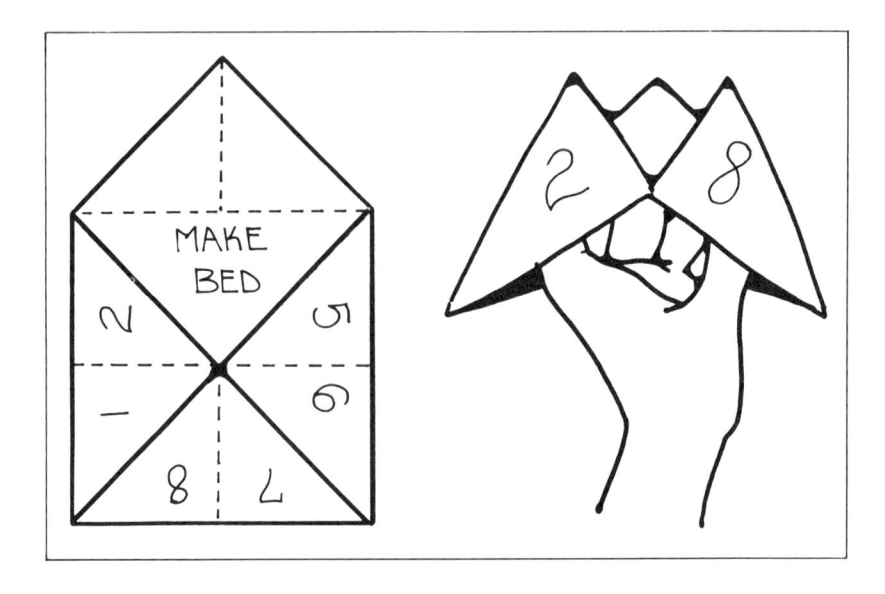

Balancing Acts. Have you ever tried to balance a marshmallow on your tongue while making your bed, combing your hair, or putting your shoes and socks on? It makes an interesting game. Older children can try to balance lifesavers on the end of toothpicks; for younger children I wouldn't suggest sharp objects like toothpicks. But all children can have fun balancing things, whether balancing something on their nose, or a book on top of their head to see how well coordinated they are.

I'm the Peanut-iest. At a given signal, everyone rolls a peanut with their nose. They roll the peanut into their room, make the bed and do the necessary jobs in that room, then roll the peanut to each consecutive room until all the tasks are completed. The child who wins that day gets to keep the peanut he rolled, and perhaps several additional peanuts, depending on the neatness of the job.

Baked Surprise. Here's another way to make enthusiastic helpers. At our house the children get up early, and we read together in the mornings, then they get dressed. After they are dressed, they have breakfast; then they can all start to do their jobs. One way to help children understand what they need to do is to wrap a list of jobs in foil and place them inside the children's breakfast muffins. As they eat their breakfast, they open up their muffin and find the lists. My mother-in-law used to put nickels and pennies in cakes and muffins for her children; so you might include a list of jobs and then a nickel or a penny inside the muffin as well. Excitement? You bet! Children can be pretty excited about the treasures they find inside their muffins.

Backwards. The children are given a list of jobs that are all written backwards. They must hold the paper up to a mirror so they can read it properly. Then they must walk *backwards* to each job that needs to be completed. When they finish the first job, they come back to the mirror and read the second job. This routine certainly adds interest to the day's work.

Secret Helpers. Take a piece of paper and write the job

that needs to be done in lemon juice or milk. The children then take it to a light and heat it a bit until the letters become visible, and they see what job they need to do. This adds a bit of mystery to the day—you might even want to call it "Sherlock Holmes Day"! You can also give each child a magnifying glass with which he can "find" ways to help in secret. That evening, family members can reveal helpful things they did that weren't noticed by others during the day.

Beanbags. This game takes a little bit of preparation, but I find that it's well worth the initial effort. With fabric pen or Artex paint, paint the symbol of a job on each of twelve beanbags (i.e., a bed indicates to a child that his or her bed needs to be made). The children can help with the drawings, too; they like to be involved and reassured that their artwork is commendable. Let them draw their concept of a certain task on a piece of plain fabric, then back the fabric with checked gingham and fill the bag with beans or wheat. When you're finished, you'll have twelve different beanbags, each representing a particular job.

It's fun to sit in the front room and have the mother throw a beanbag to each child. The child looks at the job on the beanbag, runs to complete the task, then returns and throws the beanbag back to the mother, which indicates that the job is done. Mom, it's best to immediately commend the child for doing the job; later you can check to see if it has been done neatly. If the job has been done exceptionally well, then the child might be entitled to an extra star, sticker, or a loving pat on the back. We like to applaud our family or have a family cheer. There are many small but important ways that parents can increase and enhance their children's self-esteem.

Relays. If you have four or more children in your family, you can put together an exciting relay race. After the family has been divided into two teams, a job is given to the first person in line. That person hurries to make his bed, for example, then returns and pats the hand of the next person in line, who also runs to make his bed. When the same task has been completed by all members of the team, a new job is given, and the process is repeated. The relays continue until all the work is done. It's interesting to see the "sparks" fly, and the children seem to enjoy this wholesome competition.

Simon Says. Each person in the family can take turns being Simon. Start the game with simple exercises: "Simon says stoop," "Simon says wiggle your ears," "Simon says turn your head." Then comes "Simon says make your bed," and the children hurry to make their beds. When they return, there are more fun movements—"Simon says five jumping jacks," etc., then on to "Simon says wash your face," or "Simon says let's go eat breakfast." This activity continues throughout the morning, or perhaps only for half an hour or so, depending on how long it takes each child to complete his jobs. Everyone likes to participate in this game, and everyone likes to do things well. Depending on their ages, younger children can be helped by the older ones. It makes for good physical exercise *and* efficient work habits.

Crossword Puzzles. This can be a very challenging and rewarding activity, although for obvious reasons it's better suited to older children. An example is on the following page; you'll want to use your imagination (and ask your older children to help) to come up with other puzzles that are fun and interesting for your own family. They'll help your children to understand more clearly their responsibilities in the home.

Across:
1. Each morning I will make my _____.
2. I will help my mom each and _____ day.
3. I will wash my hands with _____ and water.
4. I like to _____ the furniture.
5. After every meal I will help with the _____.
6. I like to wash my clothes and _____ my dad's shirts.

Down:
1. I will get up early and help fix _____.
7. Each morning I will hurry up, grab my clothes, run into the bathroom and get _____.
8. What I say when Mom and Dad ask me to do something.
9. When someone gives me something, I smile and say _____.
10. I always like to take my turn and _____ Mother fix supper.
11. I will show _____ to each member of my family.

Answers: Across: Down:
           1. bed   1. breakfast
           2. every   7. dressed
           3. soap   8. yes
           4. dust   9. thanks
           5. dishes   10. help
           6. iron   11. love

Allowance Versus Payday

No matter how we may try to avoid it, the subject of money always comes up when we talk about reward systems or motivational tools. Money, after all, is our society's most common medium of exchange for goods and services; and one of the most important educational tools we can provide for our children is a knowledge of how to earn money—and how to spend it judiciously. A reward system based on principles of sound money management will pay valuable dividends throughout your children's lives—and it may even teach *you* a thing or two!

It is my belief that when it comes to rewarding children for work accomplished, a "payday" system is much more appropriate and effective than the "allowance" tradition observed in many homes today. In the end, depending on how the system is managed, it may be only a semantic difference; but the concepts are important to understand so that you can make the wisest decisions within your circumstances.

The dictionary definition of the word "pay" is simply "to recompense for goods or services." Likewise, to "earn" is "to gain or deserve (salary, wages, etc.) for one's labor." "Payday," therefore, is a time at which earned wages are paid and received for labor performed.

Your children need to understand that our world is not a free-for-all. Parents go to work to *earn* the money which supports the family; they must perform certain labors to be entitled to that paycheck every week or month. Children, too, should be placed in a position where they are able to *earn* the money (and other rewards) they receive.

The word "allowance," on the other hand, is defined as "the act of allowing; a regular provision of money, food, etc." For many children, an "allowance" is a free gift, an amount of money expected and received by them each week or month, but not necessarily earned by work or other meaningful activity.

Does Mom and Dad Get An Allowance?

Now, think about it: Is Mom or Dad paid by their employer just because their name is listed in the company directory? No, indeed; they must do certain work—and do it well—to be entitled to their salary. Likewise, a child should be required to do his work well (within the limitations of his age and capabilities) if he is to "earn" his way in the family—*or in life, for that matter.* You'll find, too, that the child who is paid for his best efforts is generally a good deal more careful with his money than the child who is handed a weekly sum whether he deserves it or not.

Making Paydays Happen with A Simple Job Chart

A very effective way to create a payday for children is with a job chart (page 100). Besides listing the task, a specific amount of money is listed which they'll be paid for each completed job. This chart is simply a piece of poster board with six large boxes across the top listing Monday through Saturday. Then, down the left side are listed the jobs and their value. When the tasks are completed each day. Mom or the kids check by the job under the appropriate day of the week. Then, each week the list is totaled and a wonderful thing takes place—PAYDAY.

One of the greatest motivators that keeps the children working from their list is the same thing that keeps Dad going to work every day—a steady income. Work is seen as a means to an end, not an end in and of itself.

No one questions that work is necessary. However, the far-reaching effect of motivating children to do their work and enjoy it in the process will be well established work habits and attitudes that will be a positive part of their lives.

Keeping Motivated

There is one problem, however. Not even the most creative payday plans will keep everyone motivated indefinitely. After all, parents and children are only human. And many of us lose concentration even in things we like. If we realize this about ourselves, and if we are commited to continue in our efforts to better our homes, half the battle is won.

The other half of the battle is won by *variety*. We must keep coming up with new ways to "sell" work to our kids. If we parents don't do this, we may fail or fall way short of where we want to be.

I became aware very quickly of the need for continual "freshness" and change as I began my payday program. I then embarked on a program of trial and error, which produced a wide and wild assortment of job charts.

Not only did I concentrate on producing a variety of job charts, but I searched for fresh ways to make payday more enticing and exciting. I received the inspiration for one of my most successful approaches from an unusual source.

Coupon Paydays

Sunday newspapers have pages of "cents-off" coupons that beckon to bargain conscious shoppers. I've snipped out my share and happily took the extra time at the store and the checkstand to "cash" them in. One day while waiting my turn with a handful of coupons I got a brainstorm. The idea of "job coupons" was born.

These new job coupons would be awarded when the tasks outlined by job lists were completed. These is turn could be "redeemed" for cash from Mom or Dad—hence, a payday. But, to me, the most exciting aspect of job coupons was their

SAMPLE JOB CHART

NAME OF CHILD

"I CAN" DO IT CHART	DAILY VALUE	MON.	TUES.	WED.	THURS.	FRI.	SAT.	WEEKLY TOTAL
MAKE BED	1¢							
SET TABLE ONCE	2¢							
CLEAR TABLE ONCE	2¢							
DUST ONE ROOM	1¢							
VACUUM ONE ROOM	2¢							
PUT CLOTHES AWAY	1¢							
DO ONE THING WITHOUT BEING ASKED	2¢							
PRACTICE PIANO	1¢							
TAKE OUT GARBAGE	2¢							
MON., TUES., FRI.								
BE KIND TO SOMEONE	2¢							
WORK WITH A SMILE	2¢							
"I CARE" ABOUT MYSELF								
WASH FACE	1¢							
COMB HAIR	1¢							
BRUSH TEETH TWICE DAILY	1¢							
IF ALL THINGS ARE COMPLETE	25¢							

Reproduce this chart as a poster, with jobs you want your child to do (examples above). Then at the end of each day, mark or check those jobs that were done. At the end of the week, add up how much they earned and Presto! It's payday. A chart for each child with jobs that match his abilities is best.

flexibility. I created a whole bunch of "special bonus coupons" that were to be given to those who exhibited proper work habits and attitudes while doing their tasks. *Finally I'd found a way to measure and reward good attitudes.*

Real Value

These coupons are not only effective motivators for our children, but their use has helped me to remember to praise and recognize the kids for their efforts in helping around the house. Unfortunately, parents are quick to point out what their children do that displeases them. Many times the *good* behavior goes unnoticed and unpraised. Coupons have helped the whole family concentrate on good behavior. I especially respond to caring attitudes and willingness to help. I also praise even their smallest effort each time I award a coupon. These experiences have had a positive effect on the kids' self-esteem.

Generally, when children have good feedback at home, they say within themselves, *I'm somebody. I'm a pretty good person after all.* Kids learn these attitudes through the way parents respond to their behavior. I have seen those special *I'm pretty good after all* lights go on in my children's eyes as I've complemented them on their actions and given them grateful hugs, along with special coupons and paydays. Over the last two years that I've used these job lists and coupons, Jenny, John, and Julie have begun to develop good attitudes and work habits. And I have gained a true feeling of accomplishment and joy which has accompanied these experiences.

Implementing Coupon Paydays

When I first started using paydays and coupons, my children's enthusiasm was overwhelming. They suddenly looked upon their work as an *opportunity* instead of drudgery. Mom and Dad were able to cut down nagging nearly to zero. The kids were opting for success rather than failure. Oh sure, there were and are rough days—the kids and Mom get tired or out-of-sorts. But on the whole, the atmosphere is much more cooperative and positive.

This is how to implement coupon paydays. *First,* do a job chart without listing any money values—just write down what each child should do. Those charts are relatively easy to make for those with enough desire to try them.

Second, make your own coupons—just a few at first. I will recommend four to begin with. But first, a word about making them. I've included in this chapter examples of the coupons that have been most popular with my children and many other families that use them. You have my permission to copy them for your own personal use, within your own family. Or you may order the ones I use. For information, write or call: Raymont Distribution, P.O. Box 780, Orem, Utah 84057. Toll Free outside Utah: 1-800-453-1356. In Utah: 1-800-662-1628.

The first four coupons to start with are the following:
1. Super Jobber
2. Neato Neatly
3. Terrific Talker
4. Mighty Manners

Super Jobber and Neato Neatly are "Job Coupons." Terrific Talker and Mighty Manners are "Good Behavior Coupons."

Super Jobber. This is awarded on a regular basis. These are given to those who do their assigned jobs without being asked. This coupon is the foundation of the coupon system.

Neato Neatly. This is awarded to those who not only get their work done, but do an extra "neat" job, such as make their beds so all the wrinkles are out; sweep the floor especially clean; arrange their drawers, tidy their closets, and straighten their shelves.

Terrific Talker. This is a coupon that is awarded to those who never "talk back" or to those who don't complain or bicker. To get this coupon, a child has to say things "nice" for a time frame that Mom specifies. Some of the words that must be used are: thank you, please, yes, etc. Keep a simple tally of how many of these words are heard. When the prescribed number is reached, then the child gets the coupon.

Mighty Manners. This is a lot of fun. This coupon can

Allowance Verses Payday 103

neato-Neatly

"I'm as neat as neat can be . . . Look at my room and then you'll SEE"!

Date _____
Name _____
Point Value _____

© 1982, Suzanne L. Hansen

Terrific . . . . . . Talker

"I can talk kindly to everyone I meet . . . listen to me, what a treat."

Date _____
Name _____
Point Value _____

© 1982, Suzanne L. Hansen

Mighty Manners

"No matter when or where I eat . . . I have manners that can't be beat!"

Date _____
Name _____
Point Value _____

© 1982, Suzanne L. Hansen

104 Section Three

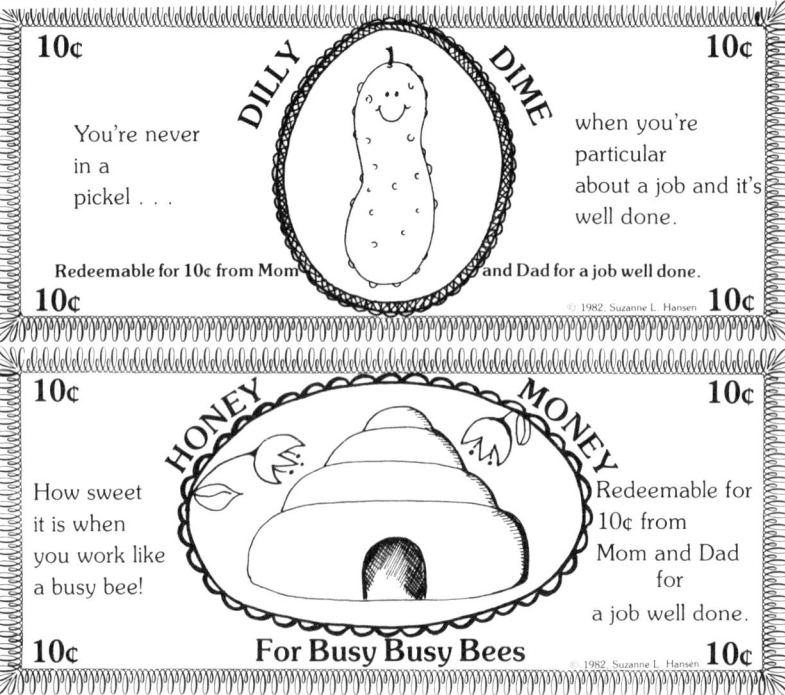

Super Jobber

Always Helps... with a smile

Date _____
Name _____
Point Value _____

© 1982, Suzanne L. Hansen

Dilly Dime

10¢ ... **10¢**

You're never in a pickel . . . when you're particular about a job and it's well done.

Redeemable for 10¢ from Mom and Dad for a job well done.

10¢ ... **10¢**

© 1982, Suzanne L. Hansen

Honey Money

10¢ ... **10¢**

How sweet it is when you work like a busy bee!

Redeemable for 10¢ from Mom and Dad for a job well done.

10¢ For Busy Busy Bees **10¢**

© 1982, Suzanne L. Hansen

Allowance Verses Payday 105

Super Sleeper

"I can go to sleep on time... Oh, it makes me feel... so fine!"

Date _____
Name _____
Point Value _____

© 1982, Suzanne L. Hansen

Super Jobber

Always Helps... with a smile

Date _____
Name _____
Point Value _____

© 1982, Suzanne L. Hansen

Super.... Sunbeam

the extra miler.

Date _____
Name _____
Point Value _____

© 1982, Suzanne L. Hansen

be received by using good manners. They are awarded for table manners and other things, such as polite behavior while traveling in the car. This coupon helps the kids remember proper manners in nearly every situation. It fortifies parents' teachings and recognizes good behavior—a positive way to encourage good habits.

Following, is a listing of job and behavior coupons that can be redeemed for cash.

Job Coupons

Busy Bucky Beaver. "You Can Leave it to Beaver." For Beavers who never leave work undone.

Mertle Turtle. She may be slow, but Mertle Turtle always gives her best.

Ollie Octopus. Always lending a helping hand. Ollies always share and care.

Hippity Hoppity Helper. Always hops to help.

Elmer Elf. Elmer Elf is for Secret Helpers. When you see something that can be done, do it and then you have a special secret if you only tell Mom. Shhh! Whisper.

Dilly Dime. You're never in a pickle when you're particular about a job, and it's well done. Redeemable for 10¢ from Mom or Dad for a job well done.

Honey Money. For busy bees. How sweet it is when you work like a busy bee. Redeemable for 10¢.

Behavior Coupons

Super Sleeper. I can go to sleep on time. Oh, it makes me feel so fine.

Super Sunbeam. For those who smile and go the extra mile by doing more then is asked.

Special Awards

These are given just for fun. The kids realize that they are not redeemable for money, but they like them just the same. We have award assemblies at dinner or as we gather in the living room. All arise to their feet and applaud enthusiastically when these awards are given. Of course, a lot of praise accompanies each award. Only a few are listed here. See the examples in the following pages.

It's Plane to See. I'm as Helpful as I can be.

Hot Diggity Dog Award. Hot Dog! What a Helper. There's a place on this coupon to write what it was awarded for.

Handy Dandy Candy Award. Awarded to those who are always sweet when being asked to help. A "sweet" treat accompanies this award.

Horatio Horse Award. Awarded for no Horse'n Around During Work Time.

How Much Are Coupons Worth?

The value of coupons can vary. I never write in an amount on the coupons. I always note at the time I award them how many points they are worth. This way I can vary the value to correspond to the task's degree of difficulty. They are also signed and dated to keep them under control.

In our family, each coupon is usually worth two points, with one point equalling one cent. I award coupons at dinner time. I prefer this time because it gives me an opportunity to recognize each child in front of the others. At other times, when things are busy, I'll sign and date the coupons and leave them on the end of their beds for a fun surprise when they awaken. I award coupons several times a week to keep enthusiasm up. However, the more that habits get established, and the more of a routine the work becomes, once a week is plenty. Once every two weeks works best to redeem them or "cash" them in.

On payday, they receive payment for their services, just like Dad does from his work. This has really prevented the whinning for candy or toys when we go to the store, because they realize that if they want something they'll soon be paid and buy it themselves. This way they don't feel like they can never get anything they want.

Until coupons get "cashed" in, they are kept in an envelope

or are stored in what we call a "coupon holder." This is made from a piece of typing paper or construction paper folded in half and then taped on either side so the top remains open. This way, it is easier for the child to put in his coupons.

The Kickoff

Before going to bed one night, I explained to the children what we were going to do the next day. I showed them their job lists and enthusiastically explained the coupons and how much they could earn.

The next morning, little Johnny, age six, got up before any one else did and completed every one of his tasks. But he didn't stop there. Without being asked, he went all over the house looking for things to do. He wanted to start on the other kids' lists. John was very motivated. To this day he is the most consistent of my children in pursuit of coupons. And at the same time is wise and generous with his money.

There's been many a day that John has made everyone's bed, vacuumed the whole house, cleared the table, and put the dishes in the dishwasher, all without having to be asked.

Jenny, age 8, has really tried, too. She's the type of person who goes the extra mile in making sure her jobs are done neatly. She continually goes through her drawers to make sure nothing is out of place. I also continue to recognize this good practice by awarding "Neato Neatly" coupons. *I love these flexible coupons.* They help me recognize the strengths of my children and assist them to develop in other areas without continual harping and nagging.

Little Julie, age four, is bubbly every time she finishes one of her little tasks, and gets a coupon, just like the "big" kids do.

The children often count the value of the coupons. Johnny once got over 350 points of Terrific Talker coupons in a two week period. His effort really made a difference in our family.

Keep the Kids Honest

When the children cash in the coupons, I rip them in half and staple them together for scratch pads; or just toss them out.

This way no child will find coupons around the house that have been previously signed and feel tempted to use them as his own. This procedure assures honesty.

Coupons can be given for many, many reasons! Coupons for good grades. Coupons good for a date with Mom or Dad, etc., etc. Once you start thinking about it, the ideas seem to fly, and you won't be able to stop them. I've been able to figure out about a hundred different types of coupons and awards that, in essence, teach children the same principles over and over again in funny, refreshingly new and cute ways.

The Greatest Motivator

We all realize, of course, that a value system based entirely on monetary rewards will never bring lasting happiness to either parents or their children. It's true that a single penny will hide the biggest star in the universe if you hold it too close to your eyes. Certainly money is important. But if the mere accumulation of money is the greatest incentive we can provide for our children, then perhaps we need to re-examine our priorities and goals as individuals and as a family.

If you have tasted the sweetness of unselfish loving and giving within your family circle, then you will understand that perhaps the greatest gift you can provide for your children is the assurance that they are valued, appreciated, and *needed* as members of your family. That "attitude of gratitude" is the all-important key that will open many doors of willing, cheerful service as your children feel appreciated for work well done. It is a rare child who will not respond positively to such loving reinforcement.

There may be days—even weeks—at a time when *no* incentive seems good enough, and you'll find yourself wondering where all those "happy helpers" went. But invariably the day will come when you're ill, or depressed, or overburdened in a hundred different ways—and you'll feel a gentle tug on your arm, accompanied by a pair of eager, innocent eyes smiling up into yours, saying, "Mom, I can help." At that moment, you'll know that all the motivating, hoping, teaching, and efforts have been well worth your while.

Easy To Make Motivational Charts

The best way to get started on anything is to do it one step at a time. Let's begin by putting our first foot forward. With your next paycheck, put aside a little for your KMK. KMK stands for *Kid Motivational Kit*. The basic kit is made up of two or three sheets of poster board, a package of colored construction paper, a roll of masking tape, a bottle of glue, a package of multi-colored markers, and scissors. All this is contained in an easy to get-to box.

After you have the basics, you can really personalize your KMK. I like to collect little "kiddie stickers." They are usually sold in stationery and office supply stores. There are all kinds of different stickers—from astronauts and stars to flowers, Miss Piggy and Kermit the Frog. I even found some that had little pickles on them for my "Dilly Do" and "You're a Dilly of a Worker" charts. I use all kinds of different stickers with my charts to measure progress, spotlight accomplishments, and add color and fun. The kids really love them, too.

Save household odds and ends for your kit. Cut out and keep the inside fronts and backs of cold cereal boxes if you don't have the funds for poster board. (The colorful drawings on these cereal boxes can also be cut out and pasted on your charts as added decoration.) *Lack of money should never stop you.* Use the kids' crayons until you can get markers or stickers. Use left-over Christmas bows and ribbon to add even more color.

I find it's easy to be more creative when I have supplies at my finger-tips. All the items in my KMK are off limits to the children, unless we are working together. This way I can keep track of these treasures I have assembled. Then, when I get an idea, I can do it "right now," because everything is handy.

However long it takes to get your KMK, set a goal to have it, perhaps in three weeks or three months, or after three paydays. You'll find that your investment will be very worthwhile.

Next, Start Thinking

Choose one of the ideas given in this chapter and think about it for a while. Start using your imagination. How can it best be applied to your family? I've given you the basics. Now it's up to you to change and adapt it to fit the members of your family.

STOP! Wait a minute! Before you go any further, I want *you* to say something out loud for me, five times: "I am a creative person. I am a creative person. I am. I am. I am a creative person." Did you do it?

Now that you've expressed belief in yourself, I know you can do anything you set your mind to do. Instead of spending valuable energy thinking of what you can't do, think of what you *can* do. Let your mind be free from all negative thoughts. I want you to learn to change yourself and your surroundings by changing your thinking as well as your children's.

We have discussed this previously, but it is such an important concept I want to put a plug in for it again.

Just Do It

We do have the power within ourselves to change our circumstances. We must first believe and then act. So get ready, get set, TRY!

Now that you've struggled and succeeded and come up with your own chart, be sure you put on a smile before you explain it to your children. Explain it with enthusiasm, and you'll find that your enthusiasm is catchy. Again, if you think it will be fun, your children will reflect your feelings. If their first response is not total joy, keep trying. Get their ideas on what they would like to try. Above all, keep your spirits up. Discover the secret of life: happiness is not in doing what one likes, but in liking what one has to do.

Do your days ever start off like this? You jump out of bed as happy as a lark. In fact, you're sure you got up on the *right side* of the bed. You get dressed and put on your best, smiling face. The world is wonderful.

You next cheerfully get your children up and kiss and hug each one. You're all excited about the day; but then, it happens. An incident or immature attitude is expressed by one or more of the children. You become provoked. You say something in a very exasperated voice, like, "If I've told you once, I've told you a thousand times . . ." Suddenly the day is upside down.

A good example of this occurred one morning in our home. My eight-year-old daughter, Jenny, woke up pretty happy. But then disaster struck. Her yellow blouse was not ready to wear with her jumper, and she couldn't find her yellow barrettes. She became very upset and spoke unkindly to me. To her, happiness seemed unreachable at that moment. Because of her frustration, I became frustrated. The other children, feeling the tension, began to misbehave. I found myself, becoming increasingly more discouraged.

Then I caught myself and said to myself: *Wait a minute. I'm not going to let my kids drag me down.*

Jenny was not able to understand, maturely, that it didn't *really* matter that much if she wore her yellow blouse or not. She could last another day and wear it tomorrow. I told myself that this "crisis" would soon be over, and everything would be fine. I decided within myself to declare my emotional independence. This was not going to be a "drag-down day," and I was going to be in a good mood, no matter what. I was determined to raise the children to my level of happiness. It worked.

Before Jenny left for school that day, she was laughing and smiling along with everyone else. I went the "extra mile" and walked to school with the kids, and we giggled and told jokes. Soon, Jenny started to see that the situation earlier hadn't been as bad as she thought. However, she would never have been able to arrive at that conclusion if I had continued to be frustrated with her.

It's Fun Being Positive
You may be asking what this has to do with charts and motivating children.

First, no chart alone will be able to turn a miserable home into a happy, cooperative one. Unhappy behavior and bad work habits are not changed as easily as the spell was broken for Sleeping Beauty. Change will surely come, however, as unhappy discouraged attitudes are exchanged for happy, enthusiastic ones. Also, you and your children will see for yourselves it is much *more fun* to be positive, busy, and productive rather than the opposite.

I Write the Story
Each new day is like starting the next chapter of an exciting novel. You're on pins and needles and don't know what's going to happen. You finish that chapter—then breathlessly, you're on to the next.

When it comes to being successful in motivating or teaching children, *one can't sit around and wait for things to happen*. I have learned that I must control how the story goes. However, within each chapter, the plot must remain flexible, for part of the story must be written as I go. But I have discovered that the more I write *before* each new day begins, the smoother things will go. Motivational job charts have helped me do this.

When I first started using job charts, they were simple lists of tasks that were checked off when each job was completed. The first really imaginative job chart I made was a real hit. I got the idea one morning when I was going through some of my craft supplies and noticed a package of little cartoon bumble bee stickers that I had purchased some time ago. The word

"Busy bee" popped into my head, and I was off.

The Busy Bee Chart

I first made a job list on half a poster board for each child. The tasks were according to my children's individual responsibilities and ages. I drew little bees all over the chart and titled it, "I'm a Busy Bee All Day." A typical chart outlined jobs as follows:

1. Make Bed
2. Get Dressed
3. Put Pajamas Away
4. Wash Face
5. Comb Hair
6. Tidy Room
7. Vacuum One Room
8. Help Set the Breakfast Table
9. Practice Piano
10. Clear Dinner Dishes
11. Help Clean up the Kitchen
12. Do Homework
13. Before Story Time, Pick up Toys, Clothes, etc.

Each day as the children completed all their jobs, they earned a bee sticker that they eagerly ran to place on their chart. Then I came up with another idea, to add more incentive.

I drew a big beehive on a poster board and taped it to the refrigerator. Above the beehive was written, "Bee the Best You Can Bee." I drew little bees flying around the hive. Each had something to say, such as, "I am a Do Bee." "I'm a Honey of a Helper." "All of us are Busy Bees." Taped on the beehive were three packages of gum wrapped in yellow paper. This was to be a sweet treat for busy bees, and a reward for each child who earned a busy bee sticker every day for a two week period. (We reduced the work load a bit on Sunday.) All three of my children were able to earn their treat. The bottom line,

I'M A BUSY BEE ALL DAY WHETHER I'M AT WORK OR PLAY!

1. MAKE BED
2. GET DRESSED
3. WASH FACE
4. COMB HAIR
5. TIDY ROOM
6. SET TABLE
7. TAKE OUT GARBAGE
8. PRACTICE PIANO

AFTER DINNER -
1 - CLEAR TABLE
2 - HELP TIDY UP
3 - PREPARE FOR BED
4 - STUDY/STORY-TIME

however, was that they had done all their jobs for two weeks and had done so, happily. I was thrilled!

The Sunbeam Chart

A chart that we have had a lot of fun with was inspired by the lyrics of a song, "You are my sunshine." This particular chart has been helpful in teaching children that they can be a ray of sunshine in the lives of others, especially members of the family.

On a piece of poster board, I drew a big sun. I then taped it to the fridge. The object of this poster was to remind all who saw it to be a sunbeam and make others happy. Each child could collect a sunbeam (a little sunshine sticker) by being kind, showing love, giving service, or by doing their jobs. For doing a certain number of these things, they could put a sunbeam by their name on the poster. It was both fun and interesting for me to see them come up to me each time they did a kind deed and tell me all about it.

The children decided together that they wanted a certain total of sunbeams by the end of a week. We wrote this total at the bottom of the chart to see how close they could come to it. It was a very high number, and they really had to work at it.

> **I'M A SUNBEAM MY NAME IS**
> _____

Then we made a second chart. This was half a sheet of poster board covered with transparent contact film. Before placing the clear covering over the poster, we wrote, "Today's Super Sunbeam," and indicated a place for a name to be written. Then, we wrote under that, "Awarded Because," and placed several long lines under this so I could write in why the child deserved to be recognized.

I usually filled this chart out around dinnertime so all could be present when we honored that member of the family. I preferred a grease pencil to write with. Crayons or certain markers did not adhere very well, and the grease pencil came off easily.

As an added incentive, I converted a mayonnaise jar into a "Sunbeam Jar." I took off the label and glued colorful material to the lid. Then on the front of the jar I taped a new label that read, "Sundrops for Sunbeams." When the children received five sunbeam stickers, they received one sundrop. The child who was honored on the "Super Sunbeam" chart received four. Also, when the child completed their jobs each day, they got a sunbeam sticker for "being responsible."

I had lots of fun with this Sunbeam theme. I draped yellow crepe paper around the kitchen and drew little sun faces and taped them up all over the house. This became a continual reminder of what we were working for. I also reminded the

Easy-to-Make Motivational Charts 119

Today's Super Sunbeam

NAME _____

AWARDED BECAUSE-
_____
_____

HOW DID IT MAKE YOU FEEL? _____

SUNDROPS FOR SUNBEAMS

children of the desired behavior by saying, "Who's going to be our Super Sunbeam, today?"

This is so much better than yelling, "Why can't you mind?" or "Why are you doing that?" or "I just can't understand why you're so bad, today." Those particular words degrade a child and make him feel less than what his is. Every child is essentially good, but they all need reminders on how they should act. Don't we all?

Kindness Kites

Here's an idea that you might want to use in the month of March. March, of course, is a time of wind and kites. Thus, the idea of "Kindness Kites" was born. I started by drawing little kites and coloring them brightly. On the front of each little kite I wrote the jobs that needed to be completed. They were then taped to a poster colored with blue sky and fluffy white clouds.

Example: Kite 1. Make bed, get dressed
Kite 2. Comb hair, brush teeth
Kite 3. Help with dishes, practice piano
Kite 4. Pick up toys, vacuum one room
Kite 5. Be sure and smile, etc., etc.

There is an alternate way to attach the kites to the poster. This method "animates" the chart. The back of a kite is "scotch-taped" to the middle of a long string. Then a hole is made in the bottom and the top of the cloud and sky poster. One end of the string comes through the top, and the other pokes through the bottom hole. Then it's tied tightly in a knot on the back of the poster. When the child completes the jobs on each kite, he pulls the string, and the kite soars in the sky, up to the top of the chart. When all the kites are flying "high," that means all the jobs are done.

After we had worked on this chart for two weeks, I prepared a special surprise for the children. I cut a kite shape out of a sheetcake, decorated it with a frosting smile and a string-licorice tail. When I produced it for dessert one night after dinner, you should have seen the faces. There is nothing

Easy-to-Make Motivational Charts 121

better than a treat to make a child feel the fun of accomplishment.

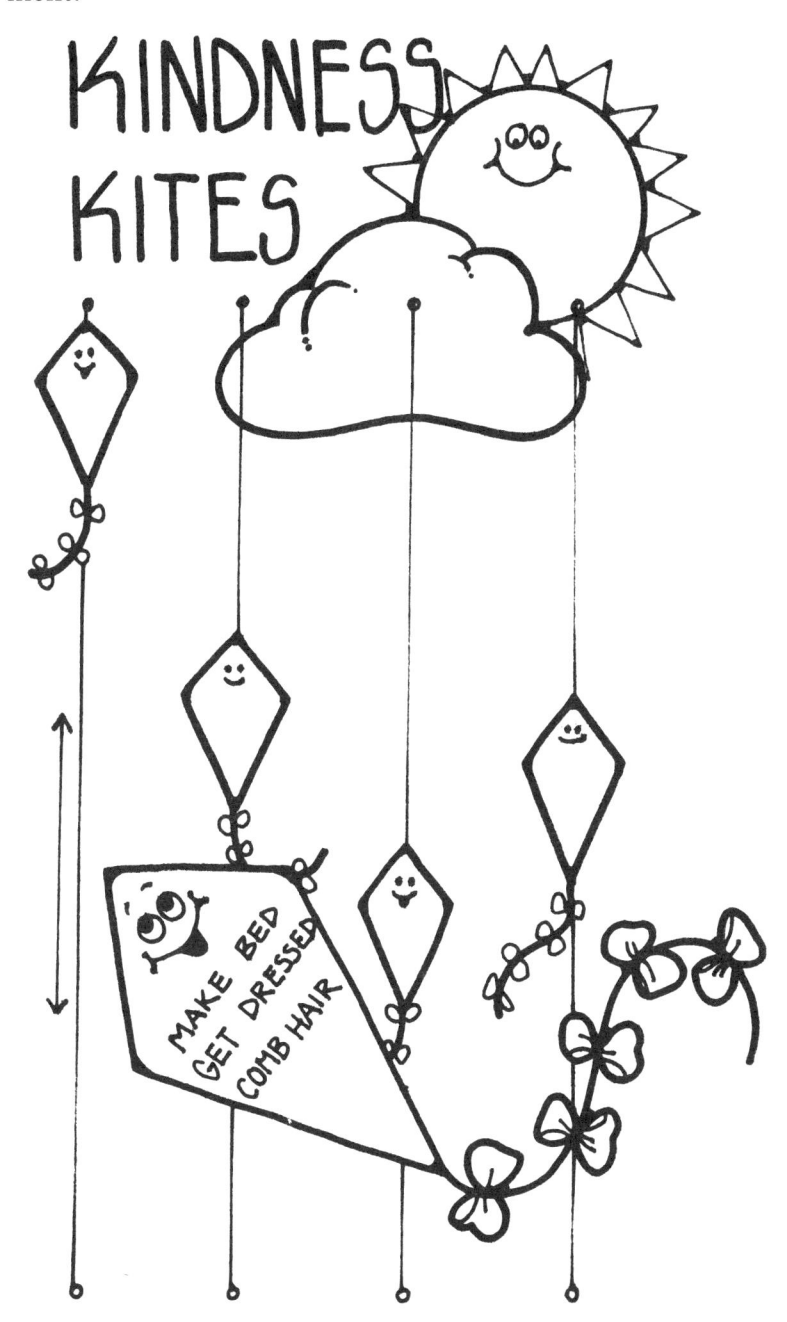

KINDNESS KITES

Kindness Coins

In March, we celebrate St. Patrick's Day. I have a fun chart that revolves around this unique holiday. I started by making a big crock of gold out of pieces of large construction paper. The crock was black. Out of gold were cut little circles which represented coins. To the side I made a rainbow out of different colored paper, coming into the crock of gold. Each time the children accomplished a task or were kind, they got to adhere a "kindness coin" to the crock of gold. We set a goal to have 85 coins before St. Patrick's Day, and we worked really hard for it. The children achieved it, and we all went roller skating together—even Dad came along. Work can produce rewards after all—and kindness, too.

A part of St. Patrick's Day, to me, has always been rainbows. I made a cute little rainbow chart for each child. On each line of the rainbow is a job or two, depending upon the age of the child. When they completed the job, each section was colored in. When the rainbow was finished, a treat was given.

One morning we had rainbow pancakes. I squirted different hues of food coloring in the batter, swirled it once, and then poured it on the skillet in the shape of rainbows. Such a simple reward, but so much fun—and the children loved it.

Easter Basket

This chart looks like an empty Easter basket. It can be drawn by you or the children. Then the eggs are cut out of construction paper, decorated, and on each, a job is indicated. As the child completes each task, he adheres the egg on the Easter basket. When the basket is full, everything is done.

These eggs can be attached by a little roll of masking tape on the back, or a very handy plastic, sticky putty that can be purchased from your local craft supply store. After the basket has been filled, the eggs are removed and stored for the next day.

KINDNESS COINS

Kindness Begins With Me!

I'M A GOOD EGG!

PICK UP TOYS

Save Your Charts

It's important that you don't waste your efforts. Your charts can be stored easily. Then when you need an idea or don't have a lot of time, you can take out one of the old charts, and it will seem brand new to a child.

The Carrot Patch

This chart can be used around either Easter time or during fall harvest. It's called the Carrot Patch. This is made from half a piece of brown-painted poster board to represent earth. Then about the middle of the chart, a horizontal cut is made about twelve inches long. From this slit the child pulls construction paper carrots that have jobs written on them.

Use Symbols for the Young Ones

On this chart, the carrots are large enough that pictures of the jobs can be drawn on them, such as a comb to indicate combing one's hair. Through these very simple symbols, young children can understand which task they should do next. A toothbrush means brush your teeth; an apple means time to eat; a dish means take your dishes to the sink; and so on. By using symbols, even three-year-olds can start to help.

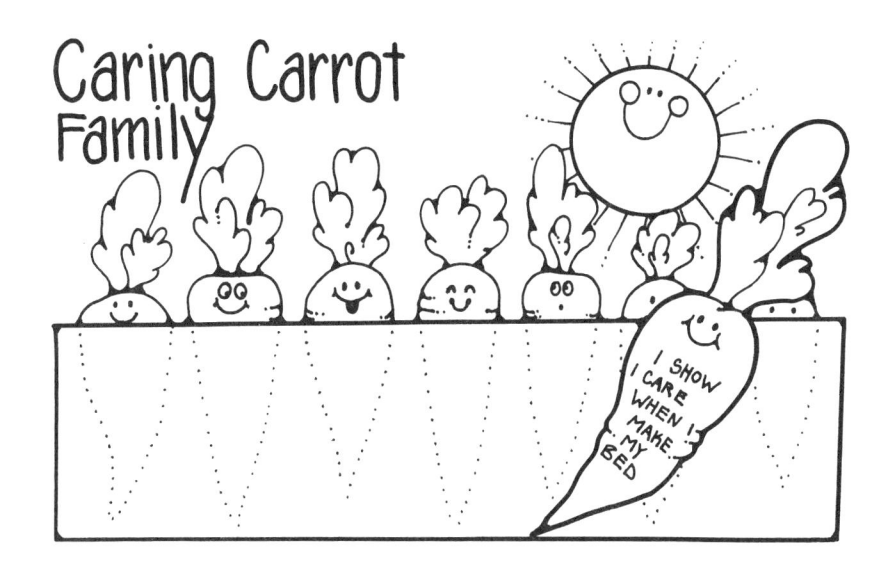

Polka-Dot Chart

This is another example of a simple symbol chart for small children. On half a piece of poster board, cut out and affix different colored construction paper circles. Tape each circle to the board at its very top so it can be lifted up. Under each circle draw a simple picture of the job to be done. My youngest, Julie, likes to do her "polka-dot" jobs in a simple little "polka-dot" apron I made her, and sing the "Polka-Dot Door" song from the T.V. show of the same name. This was a thrilling adventure for this three-year-old, and she is learning good work habits in the process.

Pizza Puzzle

To do this chart/puzzle, draw about a 12-inch circle on a piece of poster board. Then divide the circle into equal pieces of "pizza." Number these pieces (1, 2, 3, etc.) and draw the job symbols in each numbered pie section. Next, on a large piece of construction paper, make another 12-inch circle. Divide this into the exact size and number of pie sections as are drawn on the chart. On these sections, draw pizza crust and the same number of little round pepperonis to correspond to the written number of the job sections. Then have the young ones color and cut out these pizza crust sections.

Now the children are ready to use this chart/puzzle. First, Mom gets it down from a safe place and places it in front of the child on the table. Then he finds job number "one." That might be, "make bed." The child runs and does that job, then comes back to the table, finds the appropriate pepperoni number "one" that corresponds to the job number, and puts the piece over the pie section of the chart. Presto—not only is the child doing work, but he's doing a puzzle, and learning his numbers at the same time.

Butterfly Chart

This chart works on the same principle as the "animated" *kindness kites*. Jobs are written on brightly colored butterflies that climb on strings to the top of the chart when tasks are done.

We devised a fun complimentary project to enhance the use of our butterfly chart. I had some large pieces of tricot hanging around the basement so I cut out pieces in the shape of butterfly wings. I sewed them together and attached a loop of elastic to each side. This way the wings fit around the children's arms and the kids flew around the house like butterflies while doing their work. A very simple concept but very exciting and fun for a child with imagination.

PIZZA PUZZLE

HELP WITH DISHES

WORK WITH PEP!

Betty Butterfly Flies High

Be happy
Smile!
Sweep Floor
Empty Garbage
Practice Piano
Vacuum
Brush teeth
Set table
Put toys away
Get Dressed
Comb Hair
Make Bed

Ollie Octopus

Each leg or tenacle of this delightful sea creature is a job for the child to do. Example: make bed, get dressed, etc. As a child does each job, he adds another leg to the octopus by attaching it to the large body that you draw on the chart. When the child does all his jobs for a week, he gets a special treat and award which reads, "I've got to hand it to you," or "You're a Handy Dandy Helper." (See chapter on paydays and awards.)

Never "Leaf" A Job Undone

On poster board, draw a large tree trunk with bare branches. Then cut out leaves of green for summer or red and orange for fall. It was fun for our children to help prepare this chart. They got real leaves and traced their shapes. Then they cut them out, wrote their jobs on them, and affixed each to a branch on the tree.

With only the "job leaves" on the tree, there were still many bare branches. So we hit on the idea of filling the empty branches with bonus leaves. Each day when jobs were completed, each child was permitted to put a new leaf on the tree until it became full and beautiful. The kids had fun making these extra leaves by rubbing a crayon on its side over a piece of paper that was on top of an actual leaf. Thus, the texture of the leaf was beautifully transferred to the paper. Then the kids cut out these leaves and put them on the chart as a bonus when their jobs were done.

After that, I started teaching the principle of never "leafing" their jobs undone. I put up little signs all over the house like, "I make my bed and get it done." or "I brush my teeth until they shine." We also learned a saying: "If a job is once begun, never leave it 'til it's done; be a labor great or small, do it well and stand up tall."

We want our children to do all their work and "stand up tall" with pride and a feeling of accomplishment. We want the children to learn the importance of never leaving a task undone. Hopefully in later years, they'll remember some of these teachings, and the tools we used to teach them.

Going Fishing

This is more a game than a chart—but it's a lot of fun and very simple to do. First, the children drew all kinds of variety of fish, colored them, and cut them out. Then I wrote their jobs on the back of each fish. Each child had their own set of fish with their own jobs written on them. I attached paper clips to the front part of each fish. Next, I tied a magnet on the end of a string, with the other and tied it to a "fishing pole." My son especially gets a kick out of fishing for his job. In adding to the fun, I wrote little rhymes to indicate their jobs, like, "This might sound fishy but it's true. I do dishes, do you?"

Conclusion

Don't feel overwhelmed by any of the charts I've presented here. First, let me explain that the charts I've shared with you in this chapter were prepared over a period of about two years. They were the result of much trial and error.

Next, let me emphasize that I did these charts one at a time. One built on the other. The way for you to utilize this chapter and do so effectively is to pick one idea or chart that strikes your fancy and try it. Then, once this is done, and you are over the first hump, the second, third, and fourth charts will seem much easier. The ideas that start to flow then will be your own. It will become FUN both for you and your children, and you will even amaze yourself with your creativity and wisdom.

Not long ago, I was speaking to a group of homemakers about these ideas. Some ladies expressed, almost in unison, their lack of confidence in their ability to come up with ideas. To my surprise, my son John, seven years old, who was accompanying me on this particular night, raised his hand and said, "I'll tell them about some of my ideas, okay Mom?"

Johnny then proceeded to explain in his enthusiastic way about how they could draw a big lizard on a poster board. Then make a hole where his mouth is. The jobs would be written on paper bugs, and when the kids finished their tasks, they could feed their "job bugs" to the lizard. The ladies were stunned. If a seven-year-old could do it, so could they.

Now, get ready, get set, TRY!

If you have any questions or comments concerning this book or would like to learn more about Suzanne's seminars, "How To Motivate Children To Help At Home, Happily," write or call Suzanne Lindman Hansen in care of the publisher:

Randall Book
P.O. Box 780
Orem, Utah 84057
(801) 226-1162